P9-DNG-452

A SHORTER LIFE OF CHRIST

A SHORTER LIFE OF CHRIST

DONALD GUTHRIE

ZondervanPublishingHouse
Academic and Professional Books
Grand Rapids, Michigan

A Division of HarperCollins*Publishers*

A Shorter Life of Christ
© 1970 by Zondervan Publishing House
Grand Rapids, Michigan

Requests for information should be addressed to:
Zondervan Publishing House
Grand Rapids, Michigan 49530

ISBN 0-310-25441-8

Printed in the United States of America

96 97 98 99 00 01 02 / DH / 36 35 34 33 32 31 30

Contents

Preface

The subject matter of this book was written for the article on Jesus Christ in *The Zondervan Pictorial Encyclopedia of the Bible.* At the suggestion of the publishers it has been adapted and prepared for publication as a book. This involved only minor additions, which means that this book substantially represents the form and substance of the article. Its purpose is to serve as an introduction to the life of Jesus, thus paving the way for more detailed study of His life.

As far as possible, technicalities have been avoided since the aim has been to help the non-specialist to gain an understanding of the issues involved.

I am grateful for all the encouragement given to me by the publishers in this project.

A SHORTER LIFE OF CHRIST

1

Introduction

ANY APPROACH TO Jesus Christ is important. Since He is the central figure of the Christian faith it cannot be otherwise. For this reason the books about Him are innumerable and the appearance of another needs some justification. In one sense the paths have been so well-trodden that the possibility of a new approach which would bring fresh light to the subject is slight. Yet no one who has thought much about the life and times of Jesus would for that reason be deflected from making the attempt. Not only must each age produce its own interpreters, but each interpreter must make the material his own. There is, in fact, an element of danger in setting out to find some fresh method of presentation. It may lead to a distortion of the facts. The present survey makes no claim to originality, but seeks to give an up-to-date account of the background, sources and historical outline of the life of Jesus.

Any quest for the historical Jesus is faced with immediate challenges. In some quarters it is wholly out of favor to make the quest at all. It is considered more profitable to concentrate on the Christ of faith. There are certainly problems surrounding the history of Jesus and these must not be minimized. The most important of them are discussed in the following pages. But the Christian faith is a historic faith, which attaches great importance to its historic beginnings. It is for this reason that attention has been given to background and sources as a prelude to attempting some kind of outline of the life of Christ.

The faith of the early Christians developed from a sequence of historic events. This did not mean that every believer pursued historical research into Christian origins before he was in a position to believe. When he believed in Christ he believed in One who had lived and died in Palestine, historical events to which many could witness. Indeed most of the earliest Christians were people who had seen and heard Jesus and who had come to view Him in a new way as a result of His resurrection from the dead.

This means that we possess no independent assessment of Jesus from witnesses who were not affected by the power of His resurrection. Yet even if we had possessed such evidence it would have contributed nothing to our understanding of the phenomenon that, so shortly after His death, men not only came to believe in Him but derived such power from doing so that they made a profound impact on the world of their time. The only way of accounting for this remarkable phenomenon is by accepting the historical fact of the resurrection of Christ. Once this is done it will not seem improbable that the subject of so great a miracle would Himself have been the doer of many miracles of His own.

A separate chapter is devoted to a discussion of some of the problems involved in these miracles for the historian of the life of Jesus. Many attempts have been made to circumvent these miracles by rationalistic or symbolic methods, but these have arisen because it has first been accepted as a presupposition that miracles do not happen. Under such principles it would be possible to make of Jesus a man of one's own choosing, but the following survey proceeds on the assumption that He was a unique person and as such could do unique acts. This study is an attempt to recapture something of the wonder with which the early Christians viewed Jesus as their Lord and Master.

It might at the outset be objected that any attempt to produce an outline of the life of Jesus is doomed to failure, both through lack of material and through lack of certainty in the interpretation of the material which the records preserve. But some of the objections would be based on the wrong assumption that an outline is equivalent to a biography. There is no suggestion that anything in the nature of a biography is possible. It is generally necessary to have sufficient information to trace psychological developments for a true biography to be written. The gospel material has consistently defied such an approach. The activity of Jesus is concentrated into at most three years of ministry, while all the evangelists devote a disproportionate amount of space (from a biographical point of view) to the passion narratives. The spate of liberal lives of Jesus which appeared at the turn of the century aimed to produce biographical studies which could serve as a pattern for men to emulate. They failed for the simple reason that they did not provide a Gospel. An evangelical account of Jesus, in the truest sense, is far removed from the liberal Jesus and yet it is firmly based in history. In this it is sharply distinguished from the modern existential approach which is not so based. As long as it is borne in mind that the accounts which we possess are in some respects theological rather than historical in their purpose, it will not seem fruitless to attempt some reconstruction of the life of Jesus. Many approximations must be made, particularly over questions of sequence, but the overall impression of the unique personality and mission of Jesus is unmistakable.

It is not enough, however, to survey the acts and teaching of Jesus. The early church came to a new understanding of Him and this forms the basis of Christian theology. In one sense Jesus Christ is so integral to Christian thought that any discussion of Christian theology may be regarded as a commentary on His incomparable influence. The scope of the present book allows for no more than guidelines to be indicated as to the place that Jesus occupied in early Christian thought. The chapter dealing with this forms only an introduction for further exploration of the importance of Jesus Christ.

One significant matter of an introductory kind is the range of names by which Jesus Christ is known. We will deal first with "Jesus." This is the Greek form of the Hebrew "Joshua" which was borne by several Old Testament characters. It was a common name among the Jews during the time of the Lord. He is generally distinguished from other bearers of the same name by the addition of the description "of Nazareth," at least when first introduced in the narrative. Mark, for instance, after using the title Jesus Christ in the introductory statement, refers to Jesus as having come from Nazareth of Galilee (Mark 1:9). A similar procedure is followed by Matthew, who nevertheless also used the description not infrequently in the body of the gospel. In all the gospels the name Jesus is used alone in the great majority of cases. In the Acts there is a mixture of uses. When the life of Jesus is mentioned, it is usual to use the form "Jesus" alone. Frequently Jesus is identified as the Christ.

In Matthew 1:21 the Christian significance of the name is explained. It is seen as a divinely appointed name and its meaning is derived from the root idea of salvation – "for he will save his people from their sins." It was not until later in the post-Easter period that the significance of this was recognized.

The other description, that of "Christ," is of essential importance, because it at once makes an assertion about the human Jesus which differentiates Him from all other men. There had been false Christs but only one true Christ. The word represents the Hebrew Messiah which means the Anointed One, but had come to be used specifically of the Anointed of God, who was to come in fulfillment of ancient prophecies. This is not the place to discuss the variety of concepts which were current among the Jews regarding this Messianic hope. The purpose is to denote its meaning in a Christian sense. There can be no doubt that the identification of the historical Jesus with the expected Messiah was the key to the early Jewish Christian understanding of the mission of Jesus. The name Jesus Christ carries with it therefore a deep theological significance. One must consider not the bare historical facts about Jesus of Nazareth, but the interpretation of those facts.

Although Jesus or Christ or Jesus Christ were undoubtedly the most common of the names used in the gospels, a few others merit some mention. The title Lord (Greek *Kurios*) which later became attached to the other names is seldom used in the gospels. It had strong contemporary associations. It is widely used in the LXX as a name for God. In the Roman world of New Testament times it had become used in addressing the Emperor and was also employed in certain religious cults in addressing heathen gods (e.g. the Lord Serapion). Yet when applied to Jesus Christ it took on a specific meaning. It spoke of the sovereignty of Christ among His people, but it also carried with it some implications regarding His deity. It became an issue for the late first century church when Christians were required to acknowledge the Lordship of the Emperor. Many came to the conclusion that this would be disloyal to their confession of the unique Lordship of Christ. The implications of His Lordship will be brought out more clearly in the last chapter of this book.

At times Jesus was also addressed as Rabbi, because of His authoritative teaching ministry. More will be said on this in the chapter dealing with the teaching of Jesus. Similarly the names Son of man and Son of God are discussed elsewhere and there is no need to do more than draw attention to their prevalence. It is impossible to approach the life and times of Jesus without a deep awareness that He was essentially different from anyone who had preceded Him or anyone who has since lived. It is hoped that the following discussions will deepen that impression and lead to a fuller faith in Him.

2

The Background to the Life of Jesus

There has been a vast literature describing the historical background of the period of the life of Jesus. A true historical perspective cannot afford to neglect this information, which has been valuably reinforced in recent years by the finds in the Dead Sea area. Since only the briefest sketch can be given of the historical background, the developments within Judaism from a religious point of view and the political position leading to the time of the Incarnation of Jesus will have to be largely by-passed. Our concern will be the conditions which obtained during the brief span of the life of Jesus, and to this end some account will be given of the political, social, cultural and religious situation.

A. The Political Situation

The Roman occupation of Palestine had brought with it many benefits, but had incurred the implacable hatred of the Jewish people. The occupying forces were in their eyes a threat to their national heritage and aspirations. They accordingly objected most violently to the taxation system which had been introduced and which was the cause of constant irritation. Any Jew who stooped low enough to assist in the collection of any of these taxes was the object of contempt and was socially ostracized. Under the tax system a chief collector was responsible for a whole district and then farmed out the task of collecting the taxes to sub-collectors, a process which lent itself to considerable abuse and extortion.

One feature of the political situation was the considerable measure of self-government allowed to the Jews. Much of the government of Palestine was in the hands of the ruling religious party and was conducted in accordance with Old Testament principles. There was a central council (Sanhedrin) in Jerusalem and local councils in various other centers. Punishment, where possible, was administered as the Jewish Law decreed, the main method being flogging, of which there are several instances in the New Testament (note especially the case of Jesus Himself). The fact that the Jewish accusers of Jesus required Pilate's sanction for the execution of the death sentence suggests that this was the usual procedure, although in the case of Stephen it was not followed. No doubt there were many occurrences of the operation of a kind of mob law. The central Jewish council consisted of elders, chief priests and scribes, a grouping which is often mentioned in the gospels and Acts. Although there was officially only one high priest who presided over the ecclesiastical-political administration, others who had previously held office were included under the same term, as were also others who held high Temple offices (cf. J. Jeremias, *Jerusalem* II B, 17 ff.).

Within the Roman empire as a whole a fair degree of political stability had been achieved under the rule of Augustus. It was a period of great consolidation in the realm of administration and jurisdiction. The Romans found that the Jews were, however, among the most turbulent of their subjects, mainly because of their religious peculiarities and their strongly isolationist and nationalistic aspirations.

It was the policy of the occupying power to attempt to achieve some degree of adhesion among the various peoples of the provinces by absorbing their local deities into the Roman pantheon, but this policy was impossible in the case of the Jews, who possessed no image for their God. No doubt the Romans had little real understanding of the Jewish people, which was reflected in their series of procurators sent to Palestine. Pilate may be cited as an example, although he was worse than most, as is seen from the fact that the Roman authorities recalled him because of his mishandling of the situation. He committed many atrocities against the Jews which bitterly antagonized them. He took no steps to avoid offending the religious scruples of the Jews. It is no wonder that at the trial of Jesus they threatened to regard Pilate as ill-disposed toward Caesar if he let Jesus go, a threat which had considerable thrust in view of the mounting tension between the procurator and the people, and in view of the former's fear of incurring the emperor's displeasure. On a previous occasion the Jews had appealed to Caesar who had over-ridden Pilate's action. Such was the uneasy political situation into which Jesus Christ came and under which He died.

B. The Social Situation

The main points to be noted are the social structure of society generally and of the home in particular. The Jewish nation was still governed by the patriarchal concept of society. Moreover, there was considerable veneration for age, which placed the older men in a position of influence. Women and children were not favorably placed in the Jewish society. In this respect the Romans had advanced further toward their emancipation. There are incidents in the gospels which illustrate the inferior position of women, e.g. the Samaritan woman, for the Samaritans were on a level with the Jews in social structure. As far as the Law was concerned, women were not obliged to be taught the Law. Jewish education, which centered in the learning and interpretation of the Law, was provided for boys but not for girls. It is one of the more surprising features of the ministry of Jesus, although it took place in an essentially Jewish setting, that women were numbered among His followers.

In the realm of marriage there were two divergent schools of thought among Jewish teachers regarding the permissibility of divorce. The school of Hillel was less stringent than that of Shammai, the former allowing divorce for a number of pretexts in which the wife displeased the husband, while the latter allowed it only in the case of infidelity. This illustrates the fluidity of social ethics even among the Pharisees. Generally speaking, the home was an important unit in the Jewish social structure. It was a matter of social honor for a man to marry. Moreover, among the Jews there was no sanction for the widespread heathen practice of exposing unwanted babies to the elements to die.

In the time of Jesus the Jewish society was roughly divided into two groups. The religious parties, the Sadducees, Pharisees and Essenes (particularly the two former) considered themselves apart from the ordinary people. There was considerable contempt for the "people of the land" (*Ha'am ha 'ares*), particularly among the Pharisees, a factor which will be commented on when the religious situation is outlined below. From a social point of view it is important to recognize this distinct division, because it explains many of the sayings of Jesus about His contemporaries.

C. The Cultural Situation

In the northern district of Palestine there were many Hellenistic cities, in which Greek ideas and practices flourished. Not only was this true of the cities known as the Decapolis, but also of many other cities on the borders of Palestine. Something of the impact of this could not fail to affect those sections of Jewish culture which were most open to outside influence. Previous to the discovery of the Qumran literature it seemed most unlikely that Hellenistic ideas would have permeated into Jewish circles, but the Qumran community, although Jewish, was not impervious to Greek and even Oriental influences. Whereas the major currents of Jewish thought, particularly that of the Pharisees, were still resistant to the inroads of Greek culture, yet in the time of Jesus the narrower exclusiveness was beginning to break down. An interesting question arises regarding the possibility of Jesus using the Greek language in Galilee, in addition to Aramaic. No certain answer can be given, but there is little doubt that many in Galilee used Greek. In all probability the area was bi-lingual, and the possibility certainly exists that Jesus was acquainted with Greek. His teaching was certainly in Aramaic, for not only have a few of the Aramaic expressions been preserved in the Greek gospels, but Aramaic was the language of the common people, to whom Jesus mainly addressed Himself. It is not impossible, however, that Jesus was acquainted with Greek modes of thought, and it need not be considered incredible that at times He expressed His teaching in forms which would have affinity with those modes (as appears at times to happen in the fourth gospel).

D. The Religious Situation

1. *Worship Among the Jews*

In the Jewish religious outlook of the first century there were two major foci, the Law and the Temple. The Jewish people may well be described as the people of the Torah, for the teaching of the Law was normative for Jewish life. It was not just the written code of Law, but a great body of oral tradition, which for them possessed equal validity. All Jewish boys were grounded in the teaching of the Pentateuch from their earliest schooling. The book of Leviticus was, in fact, their first textbook. It was the parents' responsibility to instruct their children in the minutiae of the ceremonial Law as the various festivals came around. The synagogue services would serve the same purpose. These services comprised confession of faith, prayer, Scripture reading, address and benediction. The Scripture reading was in accordance with a lectionary, based on a three-year cycle, in which a passage from the books of the Law was linked with a passage from the Prophets. It is possible, however, that no fixed passages were set for the prophetical books in the time of Jesus, although such an arrangement is known to have been followed at a later date. The choice of reader and preacher was left to the ruler of the synagogue, who could invite anyone capable of doing it. This accounts for the number of occasions when Jesus addressed synagogue audiences. The ruler of the synagogue exercised a great deal of influence and was regarded with respect by the people. The local communities were essentially religious communities.

Although the synagogue was the center of community life, the Temple cultus exerted a powerful influence over the pious Jew for a number of reasons. The Jews of Palestine and the Jews of the Diaspora (those in regions outside Palestine) were still considered a single unit, and one important unifying factor was a common allegiance to the Temple cultus. Every year pilgrims came to Jerusalem from other parts of Palestine, and from Jewish settlements throughout the Empire, to attend the various festivals and particularly at Passover time. The Temple worship was highly organized, with twenty-four divisions of priests, who worked on a rotation system to ensure continuity and efficiency.

The sacrifices of burnt offerings were offered twice daily in the Temple, but there were many other kinds of offerings in addition. The burnt offering was significant for the people of Israel as a whole, but there were other types of offerings for individuals, whether offerings for unintentional sins, or votive offerings before some hazardous undertaking, or thank offerings for some deliverance. The Temple cultus had great relevance to the everyday life of the people. But it was at festival times that special focus was upon the Temple. Since the festivals play some part in the gospel events, it is fitting for some description to be given, especially as John makes a feature of them in his account of the activity of Jesus.

There was a festival for the New Year, but this is not referred to in the gospels, nor in fact is the Day of Atonement, observed shortly afterwards, in which the high priest alone was permitted to enter the Holy of Holies. There are several references to the Passover, which assumes particular importance for the life of Jesus, for this festival was in progress at the time of the crucifixion. It was not long before the historical connection led to the recognition of a theological link. This was indeed implicit in the institution of the Last Supper. It was customary for the Passover to be observed in homes and great importance was attached to the family unit involved. It was necessary for the family group, in fact, to remain together over the Passover night. This throws light upon the group of disciples whom Jesus had with Him for the final Passover meal, and explains why He did not leave Jerusalem that night for Bethany. In close connection with the Passover was the feast of Unleavened Bread, also mentioned in the gospels. This was held as a festival of remembrance of the Exodus, although it originally commemorated the commencement of harvest.

The most joyful festival was Tabernacles, which was popular because it involved the worshipers in dwelling in booths constructed from foliage. In the Temple courts were special illuminations and a daily ritual involving the pouring out of water. Both of these features furnished Jesus with a teaching point when He was in Jerusalem at the time of the feast (John 7:1 ff.). In John's gospel the feast of Dedication is also mentioned, but no particular significance is attached to it. The feast of Pentecost, which was a thanksgiving festival for the grain harvest, is not mentioned in the gospels, but is prominent in Acts.

It is a fair deduction that since Jesus was a Jew the Temple cultus must have had great importance for Him, a fact which is borne out by two particular occasions: the first when He questioned the doctors of the Law in the Temple at the age of twelve and regarded this as His Father's business, and the second when He cleansed the Temple of unworthy elements by appealing to what Scripture said about His Father's House.

There was one more feature which was shared by all Jews

regardless of the party to which they belonged. This was their exclusiveness. In some ways this was a beneficial feature, but in other ways not. Those tenets which the Jewish people held to tenaciously were better preserved through an exclusive policy than would have been the case had they allowed themselves to become mixed up with Gentile ideas and practices. The Maccabaean wars had been sparked off by an attempt to do this, and in the time of Jesus the Jewish people could not forget the heroism which had preserved for them the uniqueness of their faith. There were two main areas in which the Jews were superior to their heathen neighbors – in their theology and in their ethics. Their concept of God was infinitely more exalted than the idolatry of the contemporary Gentile world and caused many of the finer minds among the Gentiles to seek satisfaction as Jewish proselytes. The same may be said of the ethical ideals of Judaism, which were in marked superiority to the debased morals of the heathen religions. This sense of superiority and the desire to hedge themselves around contributed in no small measure to the intense dislike for Jews noticeable among many Gentile peoples.

2. *The Jewish Parties*

For a right evaluation of the religious atmosphere in the time of Jesus it is necessary to survey the four major groups – Pharisees, Sadducees, Essenes, and Zealots. Of these the first is the most important for one's purpose because of its more dominant religious influence and because of the frequent interchange which Jesus had with them. The Sadducees were more politically powerful, but Jesus did not find Himself so often taking up issues with them on religious matters. The Essenes are not mentioned in the gospels at all, but should not for that reason be ignored, for their very existence was a protest against the other parties, a protest with some aspects of which Jesus would find Himself in sympathy. The Zealots come into the gospel story only incidentally, although it should be noted that one of the apostles is named Simon the Zealot.

a. *A Comparison Between Sadducees and Pharisees*

It will be valuable to make such a comparison before giving more detailed attention to the Pharisees. The Pharisaic party had its rise in the movement of the Hasidim, who were opposed to the Maccabaean militarism and were devoted to a campaign to bring about repentance and spiritual renewal. Among the Pharisees this developed into a legalistic approach, which is amply illustrated by many incidents recorded in the gospels. They spared nothing in their devotion to the Law. They were committed to carry out what the scribes prescribed. It is not surprising, therefore, that at the time of Jesus the majority of scribes belonged to the Pharisees. The party was characterized by a deep religious zeal which extended not only toward the Torah, but also to the oral Law. This was the same position that Rabbinic Judaism maintained toward the Halakah, or traditional Law. Pharisaism can be rightly assessed only against this sense of devotion to a tradition which was as binding as the written code. Some of the reasons for this legalistic approach will be discussed below, but for the present it is the purpose to compare Pharisaism in these features with Sadducean ideas.

The Sadducees adhered only to the teaching of the Pentateuch and strongly rejected the Pharisaic overloading of the Law with tradition. Basically, the Sadducees were nearer to a purely Biblical approach, although it must be remembered that the Pharisees sincerely believed that oral tradition provided an adequate, indeed the most adequate, interpretation of the Mosaic Law. They were basically agreed therefore on the importance of the Pentateuch as a foundation for Jewish society.

The difference in attitude toward the oral Law led to some fundamental disagreements. The most notable controversies were over the resurrection, which Pharisees maintained, but which Sadducees denied. The latter disputed supernaturalism generally, as is seen from their rejection of belief in angels. They were, in fact, hard-headed, with a tendency toward materialism.

In Palestine in the time of Jesus they were the land-owning class, whose main interests were political rather than religious. They regarded the Roman subjugation as rather less obnoxious than their Pharisaic brethren. In matters of jurisdiction the Sadducees were inclined to greater severity of action than the Pharisees, who erred on the side of leniency for fear of unwittingly opposing truth. Gamaliel's advice of caution (Acts 5:38 f.) is typical of this approach. When the Sadducean Caiaphas was considering the threat of Jesus to the Jewish hierarchy, he displayed a devotion to political expediency which no Pharisee would have expressed so unequivocally (John 11:48). Compared with the Pharisees, the Sadducees had a lesser concept of God and a greater confidence in man, although still related to the Jewish Law.

b. *The Pharisees and Their Doctrines*

(1) *The Schools of Shammai and Hillel.* Mention has already been made of these two schools, but it is important to have a clear understanding of the difference between them when considering the attitude of Jesus toward Pharisaism as a whole. Hillel, who originally came from Babylon, maintained a liberal approach toward the Law, whereas Shammai was more rigorous. The former was probably a city man and the latter more in touch with agriculture, and this difference appears to have had some bearing on their general religious attitudes. It should be remembered that these two schools of thought virtually constituted the national Bar for local jurisdiction under the Roman constitution. Their decisions were more than niceties of Jewish casuistry, but affected the everyday running of the country.

Some examples of the differences in their rulings may be given to illustrate the fact that judgments on some issues could differ considerably. It has already been pointed out that Shammai allowed divorce only for unchastity or gross immodesty, whereas Hillel admitted it for any cause which displeased the husband. The same tendency is seen in relation to debts outstanding in the Sabbatical year. Since the Old Testament Law specified that all debts must be forgiven during that year, it became impossible for poor people to obtain loans during the previous period, but Hillel found a way around this by inventing the device known as "prosbul," which circumvented the requirement for all debts to be forgiven. This is an example of the liberalizing treatment of the Law which went to such an extent that it virtually nullified the Mosaic requirement.

The Pharisees, particularly Hillel's party, were making serious attempts to face new problems realistically. The Sadducees tended to take the view that where no Law existed on any issue, none could be made. But the Pharisees were prepared to see how the Law could be adapted to new issues. This arose from their conviction that the Law must be normative in all situations. Some of the criticisms of Jesus directed against this party were against the casuistry with which they were attempting to apply their chosen policies. It may assist in appreciating the tendency of Pharisaism to impose minute directions in all spheres of ethical conduct if it is realized that the restrictions themselves were regarded as safeguards. The common people, it was supposed, would too easily transgress the Law if sufficient barriers were not erected to hedge it around. Their casuistry was thought to possess social implications, and whereas they despised the common people as an inferior breed, they prided themselves with having their welfare at heart.

Of the Pharisees and Sadducees, the former were the most popular with the people. They shared with them a common hatred of the Romans, as against the more compromising tendencies of the Sadducees. Moreover, their doctrines and practices were respected even when they were not acted upon. They had a studied policy to court popularity, as for instance, by street corner prayers, which were condemned by Jesus for ostentation. In the light of this popularity, it may seem strange that Jesus was so strongly critical of them, but reasons will later be given why His denunciations were so strong.

(2) *The Main Tenets of Pharisaism.* A brief account of these tenets is necessary because they formed the background for some of the teaching of Jesus. Pharisaism had a high concept of God. He was powerfully active in human history, particularly in the history of Israel. This exalted concept had been pushed so far that He had become transcendental. While there was still divine activity, it was through intermediaries. The Torah had indeed become the major agency of God in His dealings with men. It was against such a view of God that the teaching of Jesus about the fatherhood of God must be placed.

It was because the Law was the expression of the eternal will of God that it became for the Pharisee the norm in all matters of behavior. Any action which contravened the Law, as Pharisees understood it, was an act of impiety and must be condemned. It was not easy for a Pharisee to accept such authoritative pronouncements as those which fell from the lips of Jesus, which went beyond the precepts of the Law. The national existence was so bound up with observation of and loyalty to the Law that the Pharisees could not accept that any personal authority could abrogate or even modify the official understanding of the Law.

It is not surprising to find that Pharisees were addicted to pride. Their theology centered not only in the superiority of

Israel over other nations as special objects of God's favor, but also in the additional favor shown to those whose piety was proved by exceptional devotion to legal observance. It is the very nature of legalism, with its emphasis on human achievement, to engender pride.

Another feature of Pharisaic belief was acceptance of the immortality of the soul, the resurrection of the body and future retribution. Those eligible for resurrection, according to Josephus, seem to have been restricted to the righteous. Since the Sadducees denied the resurrection altogether, it is evident that in the realm of eschatology Jesus stood nearer to the Pharisees. For the latter the future world judgment was regarded as the consummation toward which all human history was moving. This accounts for the absence of the same materialistic and political considerations, on the part of the Pharisees, which were so dominant with the Sadducees. The idea of the end *(eschaton)* played no inconsiderable part in the teaching of Jesus.

When the Messianic beliefs of the Pharisees are examined, it is not easy to form a consistent picture. There was frequent use of both the titles, Messiah and Son of David. These show the expectancy that one would come to occupy the throne as King in Israel. This Messiah was to be anointed by God, raised up to lead the people in righteousness. It was as much a spiritual as a political concept; it had inevitable political overtones, since Israel was itself a theocratic nation. Various opinions existed concerning the nature of the Messiah to come. Some thought in terms of a heavenly being, others in terms of a warrior king. None ever supposed that the Messiah would be rejected by His people. It was for this reason that the notion of a suffering Messiah was a great stumbling block to the Jewish people. The bare idea of a suffering Messiah was not completely unknown, but where it existed it was in the sense of chastisements encountered through fidelity to the Law, and in any case it did not belong to Jewish beliefs in the time of Jesus.

Many of the rigid ceremonial requirements imposed on the Pharisees were aimed at preserving ritual purity. The detailed requirements had obscured the original purpose of the Law, which merited and received the severest condemnation of Jesus. Yet, it is important to note that at no time did He condemn their sincere desire to fulfill the Law. He made it clear that He Himself had not come to destroy the Law but to fulfill it.

It will be seen that whereas there is much in the actions and teaching of Jesus which would not have conflicted with the Pharisaic ideals, the unique approach of Jesus would lead to a direct confrontation with cherished traditions, and the many controversies recorded in the gospels are therefore not surprising.

c. *The Essenes*

Until the discovery of the Dead Sea Scrolls, knowledge of this group came mainly from Philo, Josephus, and Pliny. Most scholars are convinced that there is a close relationship between the Essenes and the men of Qumran, although there are some who seriously dispute this. The Qumran community may well have been a special sect within the Essene movement, which would account for the similarities and differences between the evidence from the scrolls and that from Josephus. The main divergences concern the regulations for admittance.

The Essenes were a separatist group who regarded the Jerusalem Temple worship as corrupt. Their monasticism was therefore essentially a protest. They were as devoted to the Law as the Pharisees, but in a different way. They were, in fact, more stringent. There were rigorous rules for the government of the group, as the *Rule of the Community* or *Manual of Discipline* shows. There were severe penalties for any offense against the community. The organization was equally rigid, but the details need not be repeated. The purpose is to show what possible contribution the Qumran evidence can make to the understanding of the mission of Jesus, and the following considerations may be noted:

The absence from the gospel records of any reference to contact between Jesus and the men of Qumran is not surprising. Qumran was essentially a monastic order to which men withdrew to escape involvement in the contemporary Jewish world. The ministry of Jesus, therefore, passed it by. Yet the movement points to a real dissatisfaction within Judaism with current religious life and enables a better understanding to be made of the protests of Jesus Himself against the Pharisees and Sadducees. Moreover, the teaching of Jesus in some aspects possessed greater affinity with Essenism than with the other groups. As far as the Essenic doctrine is concerned, an interesting factor was the belief in two Messiahs, a Messiah of Aaron and a Messiah of Israel. Since the Messiah of Aaron takes precedence, it no doubt arose from the conception of Qumran as a priestly community. In itself the Messianism of this community contributes little to the understanding of the Messianic claims of Jesus.

Of more importance is the place of the Covenant in the community. The members were men of the New Covenant, and each man had to signify annually his allegiance to it. It was really a reaffirmation of the Old Covenant which contrasts with the New Covenant inaugurated by Jesus. His presentation of the Covenant was in line with the prediction of Jeremiah (Jer. 31).

There has been much discussion regarding the Teacher of Righteousness who is often mentioned in the Qumran literature. He may well have been the founder of the community. He was certainly highly esteemed, especially for his expositions of Scripture. Some scholars (such as J. L. Teicher), maintain that the title is describing Jesus, but this view is generally discounted. Unlike Jesus, the Teacher of Righteousness was not regarded as the subject of Old Testament prophecies, nor was he regarded as the Messiah. Although no connection can be established, the striking parallel between this Teacher and Jesus the Teacher, who came to impart righteousness, cannot pass unnoticed. It shows that there were elements in Judaism which were reaching out toward greater purity.

The men of Qumran were deeply conscious of forces opposing the truth, as is seen particularly in the references to the Wicked Priest. It is also apparent in the strong antitheses which are found in the modes of thought. The community members are sons of light engaging in battle with the sons of darkness. Truth is in conflict with error. This is of special importance as a background against which to place the Johannine portrait of Jesus. No longer can the antitheses which are so characteristic of John's gospel be ascribed to Hellenism, without taking fully into account the syncretism which before the time of Jesus had already taken place within the Essene branch of Judaism.

d. *The Zealots*

These belonged to a religious-political movement which opposed payment of tribute to a heathen emperor on the grounds that allegiance was due only to God. The movement began as a revolt in A.D. 6 under Judas the Galilean and continued its activities until after the siege of Jerusalem. It played an important part in resistance against the Roman occupation. Its last stronghold, Masada, fell in A.D. 73. One of the Twelve Apostles is named Simon the Zealot; whether the adjective was added simply to describe his zeal or as an indication of his association with the political party is not known. The theory that Jesus Himself was associated with the Zealots (so S. F. D. Brandon) may be discounted, not only because it lacks evidence, but because it is impossible to interpret the words of Jesus as the words of a political enthusiast. Jesus left Rome severely alone. His mission was spiritual, not national.

3

Various Approaches to the Life of Christ

It has already been pointed out in the opening chapter that it is not possible to reconstruct a biography of Jesus in the modern sense of the word. The available data are quite insufficient. This chapter will be concerned with the various theories which have had vogue among different schools of thought, with special emphasis on the problems raised by modern debates concerning the historical Jesus. In the brief compass available it is possible to give only the main lines of debate. Yet this will be sufficient to present a brief summary of the various approaches without which no true assessment of the relevance of Jesus Christ for modern times would be possible.

A. The Traditional Approach

Although the available sources are insufficient to construct a biography of Jesus in the modern sense of the term, the traditional approach to the sources has always maintained that the data are adequate for some appreciation of the Jesus of history. It had always been assumed, until the rise of eighteenth century rationalism challenged it. The large amount of space devoted to the passion and resurrection narratives was no problem for those who saw no discrepancy between the historical Jesus and the Christ of faith. Primitive Christian belief fastened on the importance of Christ's death and resurrection, abundantly proved by the Acts and Epistles within the New Testament. The apparently lopsided arrangement of material in both the synoptic gospels and in John bears witness to the major content of the early Christian faith. It was not unreasonable to suppose that if so important an element of faith was accurately reflected in the evangelist's arrangement, the rest of the material should be regarded as equally historical.

Certain difficulties were nonetheless recognized. Some explanation had to be given of the instances where apparent disagreements occurred within the synoptic gospels or between the synoptic gospels and John. The traditional approach to such problems was harmonistic. Since it was maintained that there could be no discrepancy within the inspired records, it must be possible to reconcile apparent contradictions. Many of these harmonistic attempts were more ingenious than convincing. When, for instance, it was maintained (e.g., by Osiander) that Jairus' daughter must have been resurrected more than once because the incident is placed in a different sequence within the synoptic gospels, the improbability of such a solution becomes at once apparent. It was the weakness of much of the traditional approach to the gospels that it tended to over-stress some feature, such as the order of events, without sufficient examination of the validity of the basic assumptions. Dogmatic considerations were more important than historical, with the consequence that the older traditionalists exposed themselves to rationalistic attacks. Until that time there had been no question about the validity of the miraculous. The Christ of faith was so deeply entrenched in the religious concepts that it was perfectly reasonable to suppose that He had power over the natural world to such a degree that in His hands the abnormal became normal.

The advantage of such an approach is obvious. All the gospels may without question be treated as historical sources and the main preoccupation of any scholar producing an outline of the life of Jesus is to discover the best method of harmonizing the accounts. Since John's account presupposes a longer period of ministry than the synoptics, it has been the usual procedure of traditionalists to fit the synoptic outlines as far as possible into the Johannine structure. This traditional approach to the sources has been attacked on several fronts during the last century and a half of criticism. It is essential to have some insight into the grounds for these attacks to appreciate the position of modern criticism in its approach to the historical Jesus.

B. The Rationalistic Approach

Rationalism showed its attack upon the gospel material in the deistic renunciation of miracles as support for Jesus' claims to messiahship. This antipathy toward the miraculous has been characteristic of rationalism ever since and has affected many schools of thought which have had little in common with the basic tenets of deism. It was an attack on the supernatural element, and once the miraculous was pronounced either impossible or suspect it was essential to view with suspicion other elements in any sources which treated the miraculous as normal. This was the starting point for German critical appraisals of the historical Jesus. Whatever in the gospels did not square with the assumption that the supernatural interpretation of the life of Jesus was impossible, must be excised from the records as later interpolations. Such was the rationalistic impact on the sources of the life of Jesus. It was not surprising, therefore, that the nineteenth century was to see a whole crop of unhistorical "histories" of Jesus, many of them almost wholly fictitious.

Before the dawn of the nineteenth century H. Reimarus had produced a book in which he regarded the resurrection of Jesus as an invention of the apostles, who themselves inaugurated a community to await the return of Christ. To avoid possible exposure they stole the body of Jesus. This kind of approach won no support in Reimarus' own time, but was a precursor of the eschatological theory of A. Schweitzer more than a century later. Reimarus made no attempt to come to grips with the Johannine problem. He preferred the synoptic gospels and imposed his fraud theory on them. During the nineteenth century many others were either to reject or to ignore the Johannine account.

Attempts were next made to write historical accounts of Jesus from the standpoint of the contemporary climate of opinion. There was no hesitation in making Jesus speak as nearly as possible in rationalistic forms. Modifications of both sayings and events were unrestrained. Representatives of this tendency were J. J. Hess and F. V. Reinhard. Another who illustrates the awakening of the critical faculties in relation to the sources of the life of Jesus is J. G. Herder, who considered it to be impossible to harmonize the synoptic gospels with John, and who treated the latter as something of a protest against the former.

It was H. E. G. Paulus who presented the most thorough-going rationalistic approach to the gospels, for he regarded the miracles as due to the eye-witnesses' ignorance of the laws of nature. This left him free to explain away the miraculous. Such incidents as the raisings of the dead were described as "deliverances from primitive burial." This is even alleged of the resurrection of Jesus. His basic skepticism has often since been reflected in other theories.

A rather modified view of the gospel miracles is seen in the life of Jesus written by K. Hase, for he had a higher regard for the Johannine miracles than those of the synoptics. Again the impossibility of accepting both accounts is assumed. A similar position was taken by F. E. D. Schleiermacher. Although less avowedly rationalistic than Paulus, he nevertheless shows the influence of the latter upon him in his explanation of the resurrection as recovery from a state of suspended animation. None of the synoptic gospels, in his opinion, presents historical facts. There is no doubt that his view of these gospels was governed by his preconceived idea of Christ.

C. The Mythological Approach

It was the radical criticism of David Strauss which marked a turning point in German approaches to the life of Jesus. He followed Hegel's philosophy and this governed his attitude to the sources. He was not hesitant to interpret the events mythologically. Anything inexplicable to Strauss was treated as myth. It is not surprising that the result was radical. Many of the mythical elements he traced to Old Testament motives. John's gospel he regarded as apologetic and therefore inferior to the others. But the latter contained much composite material due to the influence of the church upon the tradition. Although his opinions were too radical for his own age, they set the pattern for later developments, both in the views of liberal critics and in the ideas of the later form critics.

Strauss' skepticism bore some fruit in the radical opinions of Bruno Bauer, who treated John's gospel as an artistic product, and then transferred similar principles of criticism to the synoptic gospels. His conclusion was that the records were the conceptions of evangelists woven around the historical personality of Jesus. After an interval Bauer reached the logical conclusion of denying the historicity of Jesus.

D. The Sentimental Approach

Ernest Renan's life of Jesus may be described as imaginative rather than skeptical. It was certainly not historical, for Renan appealed to aesthetic taste rather than to fact. He treated the whole story as a dramatist would a play. The Jesus he produced was a Jesus of his own creation.

E. The Liberal Lives of Jesus

The heyday of liberal criticism produced its crop of interpretations, the purpose of which was to discover and present the historical Jesus apart from the dogmatic presentations of Christ. A typical example of this point of view may be found in H. Holtzmann's book on the synoptic gospels. In this he propounded a theory for the life of Jesus based on Mark, in which he drew a distinction between the earlier period of success and the later period of decline. This idea exercised a strong influence on the liberal lives of Jesus during this period. Holtzmann was not adverse to drawing from both the synoptic and the Johannine traditions.

Adolf Harnack's interpretation of Christianity was governed by his acceptance of the so-called historical figure of Jesus of Nazareth whose main function was to found the Kingdom of God on earth, and whose death did no more than set the seal on this mission. The result was that the portrait of Jesus was conformed to the contemporary pattern of nineteenth century life. In spite of the attempt to arrive at a historical presentation, the principles of criticism which these liberal scholars followed did not enable them to produce an objective account. It must be recognized that these principles were affected by the earlier rationalism, the attempt to pass all the gospel material through the sieve of what is intelligible to reason. Yet, there can be no doubt that these liberal interpreters of Jesus were convinced of the historicity of their account. Christianity became a matter of conformity to the ethics of Jesus, and by that fact it had ceased to be a gospel.

F. Various Nineteenth Century British Approaches

Some British scholars followed closely in the wake of German criticism, of whom the most notable was perhaps F. W. Farrar, *The Life of Christ* (1886). There was no tendency to discriminate between the synoptics and John, as among the Germans, although the emphasis was essentially upon the Jesus of history. Among the more conservative works may be mentioned the valuable work of A. Edersheim, *Life and Times of Jesus the Messiah,* (1883), which provided many insights into the Jewish

background and is the ablest attempt to integrate the synoptic and Johannine traditions. He made no attempt to differentiate between the Christ of faith and the Jesus of history. In much the same vein may be mentioned W. Sanday's article on Jesus Christ in Hasting's *Dictionary of the Bible*. These British representatives at the close of the nineteenth century show how little the German movements had affected the mainstream of opinion relating to the historical Jesus, but the twentieth century tells a rather different story.

G. Twentieth Century Viewpoints

1. *The Eschatological Movement*

Albert Schweitzer's book, *Von Reimarus zu Wrede* (1906), translated into English under the title of *The Quest of the Historical Jesus* (1910), created a sensation. It gave a penetrating analysis of the inadequacies of the rationalistic and liberal approaches and then presented the theory that only from an eschatological point of view could a true history of Jesus be written. Schweitzer's eschatology was of his own making. He conceived that the dominating factor in the history of Jesus was his firm belief in the imminent establishment of the Kingdom. He rejected Wilhelm Wrede's idea of the Messianic secret (*Das Messiasgeheimnis in den Evangelien* [1901]), and maintained that Jesus' hopes were frustrated. The cross was the failure of the mission of Jesus. All that remained of the Jesus of history was the example of His noble purpose which never came to anything. Even the ethics of Jesus was only an interim measure and therefore possessed no abiding validity.

Schweitzer's counterblast to the liberal Jesus was no less unhistorical. His strange eschatological blunderer was not the Jesus who lived and taught in Palestine. The difference between Schweitzer and the liberals was that whereas the latter sought to dress Jesus in modern garb, the former sought to put Him back into a first century wholly apocalyptic milieu. Neither viewpoint came to grips with the real problem of how their interpretation of Jesus contributed to an understanding of what came to be the place of Jesus in the historic Christian faith. There is no doubt that Schweitzer's hypothesis gained more support than it would have done because of the aridity of the previous liberal theories. As Hugh Anderson has said, "By his tremendous stress on the non-advent of the Parousia, for the

inauguration of which and for nothing else Jesus died in vain, Schweitzer helped to pave the way for recent versions of the primitive Church's Christology which left no place therein for faith in the historical Jesus as the decisive revelation of God for the past as well as for the present" (*Jesus and Christian Origins* [1964], 21, 22).

2. *The Dialectical Approach*

Another major twentieth century trend is seen in Karl Barth's dialectical theology. This movement was contemporary with that of Rudolf Bultmann in its origin. Both men were reared in the same theological climate, both being taught by the same liberal teachers. They both belonged to the *Religionsgeschichte* (History of Religions) school, which believed in the broadest basis for the study of the life of Jesus in the context of an examination of comparative religions. Those who exercised most influence upon both Barth and Bultmann were determined to eliminate from the sources of the life of Jesus whatever belonged to the dogmatic theology of the Christian church. These liberal scholars concentrated on the immanence of God in Jesus in a way which saw in Jesus only the exaltation to the highest possible degree of what is potential in every man. There was an absence of all thought of the divine transcendence of Jesus, and it was this that challenged Barth.

In one sense, Barth has not entered into the literary problems surrounding the sources of the life of Jesus, but he strongly reacted against the liberal idea of the historical Jesus. By concentrating on the New Testament texts and rejecting the possibility of going behind them, Barth went some way toward counteracting the approach to the texts which characterized the earlier critics. Barth's doctrine of the Word within Scripture allowed him freedom in his treatment of the biblical text. What he insists upon is a theological rather than a historical exegesis. Any attempt to reconstitute the historical Jesus as the liberals had done is no part of the Christian faith as Barth understands it. Yet he does not dispute that the object of the church's faith must be related to the past. Jesus was distinctive as compared with other men "in His inescapability, in His critical function, in His unforgettable lordliness, in His irrevocability which bursts and transcends all the limits of His life and time" (*Church Dogmatics* IV, part 2, 156 ff.). This is not the place to expand on

the theology of Barth. It suffices to show that Barth differs from his contemporary Bultmann in by-passing the problems of literary origins, with which the latter has been so closely concerned in his reaction to the same liberalism in which both were reared. Bultmann has retained more of the essential spirit of liberalism than Barth.

3. *The Form Critical Approach*

Bultmann's position must be considered within the context of an examination of the whole form-critical movement, of which he is representative of that section which attaches least historical validity to the sources. Form criticism is a movement which derived its main impulse from the failure of a rigid application of source criticism to solve the problems of the gospels. It was a method which had previously been developed to get behind the sources proposed for Old Testament criticism.

H. Gunkel's attempt to reduce the pre-literary oral material to some sort of classification by means of different forms in which the material was preserved provided a method which appeared serviceable for New Testament criticism. The most that source criticism could do was to posit sources which were no earlier than thirty years after the events related, and it was naturally considered important to attempt to fill in the gap. The main objectives were still within the field of scientific historical enquiry. Form criticism as a literary discipline belongs essentially to the period of liberal approaches to the life of Jesus, although in some of its developments, most notably in the hands of Bultmann, it became a tool to be used against the concept of the historical Jesus. This was possible because Bultmann went beyond the purely literary idea of form criticism and developed from it the form-historical method. To make clear this important distinction, the two main schools of form criticism will be considered, irrespective of the chronological development, classification being dependent on whether it is used to support historical evaluation or not.

The real focus of attention was upon Mark's gospel. It had been assumed by the Jesus-of-history school that Mark's account was basically historical and that whatever material could be fitted in from the other synoptic gospels was acceptable. The liberal representation of Jesus was therefore very much tied up with Mark's gospel. When Wrede challenged the historicity of

Mark by his theory of the Messianic secret, the whole hypothesis of the historical Jesus was also challenged. Wrede maintained that Mark had preserved no chronological sequence and that the material of the gospel had originally existed as unconnected units. Whatever unity there was in the record had been imposed upon it by Mark, who had made it appear that Jesus claimed to be the Messiah and was recognized as such by the disciples, although in Wrede's view this did not happen until after the resurrection of Jesus. The stage was therefore set for a more radical re-interpretation of the gospel narratives in the light of editorial processes which were conditioned by the Easter event. This particular trend was to play an important part in Bultmann's theory of form criticism.

The unitary view of the Markan material was further stressed by such scholars as J. Wellhausen (*Einleitung in die drei ersten Evangelien* [1905]) and K. L. Schmidt (*Der Rahmen der Geschichte Jesu* [1919]). The former contended that Mark's gospel was overlaid by editorial additions, which it was necessary to excise if the historical material was to be laid bare. The latter maintained the unreliability of Mark's chronological and geographical data and consequently challenged the possibility of producing a connected account of the life of Jesus.

In 1919 Martin Dibelius published a book entitled *Die Formgeschichte des Evangeliums* in which he analyzed various forms of gospel material according to the use to which it had been put in the period of oral transmission. Since this was essentially a missionary period, Dibelius found the *Sitz im Leben* (the situation in the life of the Church) of the various forms in the needs of the different types of church workers – preachers, teachers, and narrators. Such forms as paradigms, short narratives concluding with an important saying, would be valuable for preachers, while teachers concerned with the catechizing of new converts would use sayings which were unattached to narratives and varied in subject matter, which would be matched to the practical needs of the communities. Narrators would relate tales, often of a supernatural character, which were either created by or at least embellished by the narrators. Other categories of forms proposed by Dibelius were legends and myths, the first being material about holy people paralleled in secular writings; and the second, material in which some mythological interchange took place (e.g., the Temptation and the Transfiguration). It will at once be seen that the sources for the life of Jesus have therefore been subjected to influences which have introduced many non-historical elements. Nevertheless, Dibelius did not, as Bultmann did, deny the possibility of an historical account of Jesus. At the same time, his postulation of different classes of people using different forms of material is highly unlikely and accordingly weakens his theory. Moreover, it is clear that he has done more than classify the forms; he has evaluated them and in so doing has used his own criteria. The miraculous element is not attributed to the supernatural but to the composition of the storytellers, who wished to heighten the appeal of the tales they were telling.

A more moderate approach may be seen in the work of M. Albertz, B. S. Easton, and Vincent Taylor. Albertz (*Die synoptischen Streitgesprache: ein Beitrag zur Formengeschichte des Urchristentums* [1921]) admitted that the church had adapted the original traditions, but nevertheless strongly maintained the possibility of arriving at a concept of the historical Jesus. It is important to note that German criticism had other voices contemporary with Bultmann which did not agree with his approach toward history in the gospels.

B. S. Easton (*The Gospel Before the Gospels* [1928]) treated form criticism essentially as a literary discipline. Although he admitted that the traditions had been influenced by ecclesiastical and apologetic motives, he declined to use the classification of forms in the assessment of the historicity of the material.

Vincent Taylor (*The Formation of the Gospel Tradition* [1935]) is a representative of that school of form criticism which sees a limited value in the discipline, but is strongly opposed to the skepticism so characteristic of Bultmann's theories. He rightly calls attention to the existence of eye-witnesses which must have exerted a powerful restraining influence upon the creation of non-historical elements in the tradition and provided some guarantee of the historicity of the material which has been preserved. It is significant that Vincent Taylor declines to accept the right of form critics, on the basis of their method of criticism, to deny the miraculous. The determination of the validity or otherwise of the miracle stories belongs not to the literary but to the historical critic. Compared with the exponents of radical form criticism, Vincent Taylor is moderate, for he believes in the actuality of the historical Jesus. In fact, his trilogy on

Christ (*The Names of Jesus* [1953], *The Life and Ministry of Jesus* [1954], and *The Person of Christ in New Testament Teaching* [1958]) shows an approach which seeks to combine the Jesus of history with the Christ of faith. Such moderate use of form criticism clearly puts him in a different camp from Dibelius and Bultmann.

The same may be said of some other British scholars who have partially used form critical methods, while at the same time rejecting some of its assumptions. C. H. Dodd, (*New Testament Studies* [1953]) for instance, staunchly maintains the reliability of the chronological structure of Mark on the grounds of the evidence of Acts, which counteracts the notion of Mark as a collection of disconnected units. When using form criticism, his main interest is to discover how far the different forms can be employed in verifying the historicity of the material. Although he does not conclude for the historicity of all the material, he sees beneath the interpretive elements a substantial basis of historic fact. He seems to stand midway between the older liberalism and the newer Christ-of-faith school.

Another in the same tradition, but even more insistent on the historicity of the Markan account, was T. W. Manson (*Studies in the Gospels and Epistles* [1962]). He not only maintained the reliability of the Markan outline, but vigorously resisted the skepticism of the radical form critics. He correctly pointed out that there was less credibility in the form critical suppositions than in the gospel accounts. He believed that it was possible to arrive at the facts of the life of Jesus from the gospel sources and to make some kind of chronological reconstruction. He did not, however, cling to a purely historical quest, for he recognized that a historical reconstruction would be meaningless apart from the early Christian belief in Jesus as the object of faith. He was reluctant to create an antithesis between history and faith.

4. *The Existential Approach*

It was quite different with Bultmann, whose dissatisfaction with the liberal attempts to produce a history of Jesus turned his attention toward the Christ of faith. It will be necessary to consider his point of view in more detail since it has had a profound influence over European thought regarding Jesus Christ, and has not lacked support in British and American circles. Bultmann's approach to the records is via the *kerygma*, i.e., the proclamation of the resurrected Christ. It would not be true to say that Bultmann denies the historicity of Jesus, although he comes nearer to this at times than he himself is prepared specifically to admit. He considers that all that can be asserted without question is the "thatness," the bare fact, of the cross of Christ. It is difficult to think intelligibly of a bare "thatness" which is unrelated to a historical personality of whom at least something can be historically known. In any case, this is a different kind of *kerygma* from what the early Christians proclaimed. Nevertheless, Bultmann has performed a valuable service in drawing attention to the problem of the connection between the historical Jesus and the Christ of faith, even if his own solution proves to be totally unacceptable. The Jesus of history can become a living factor in each era of the Christian Church only if it is possible to establish the connection between Him and the faith of each era. Bultmann's probing goes deeper than that, for he maintains that since no connection is possible, there is no point in pursuing the historical Jesus at all. Cf. for Bultmann's views, his *Jesus and the Word* (Eng. tr. 1926) and *Form Criticism* (with K. Kundsin, Eng. tr. 1934).

a. *Influences Upon Bultmann*

(1) *The History of Religion School.* To understand Bultmann's methods it is necessary to be aware of influences which have had a share in the moulding of them. The liberal background to which he belonged was dominated by Reitzenstein's theory that primitive Christianity drew much from the mystery cults (*Die hellenistischen Mysterienreligionen* [1927]), and by Bousset's *Kyrios Christos* (3rd. ed. 1926), which maintained that Jesus was Lord, not Messiah, to Gentile Christians. While these theories had more effect on Bultmann's approach to Pauline theology, they are not unimportant for his theory of gospel origins, since, if true, they must find a place in his idea of the *kerygma* among Gentile Christians.

Acceptance of the view that mystery religions and Gnostic myths were a moulding factor in early Christian doctrine disposes the exegete to search for pagan parallels to account for the form, if not the content, of some of the gospel materials. Careful examination, however, shows that most of the parallels are tenuous. Can it be accepted as a legitimate method of exegesis to attribute anything remotely resembling a pagan parallel to such a source? Reitzenstein's evidence is drawn from a much later period, which makes it difficult to place any reliance upon it. As far as Gnosticism is concerned, when this became a powerful second-century movement, it met with strong resistance from the Christian Church. Had there been a close kinship between it and Christianity, it is impossible to see why this kinship was unrecognized.

Any presupposition of a distinction so radical between Palestinian and Hellenistic Christianity must inevitably affect assessment of historical data. The presupposition is unsupported by adequate evidence. The most damaging objection is the failure to recognize the uniqueness, not only of Christ Himself, but of the Church whose faith was based in Him. This was the ineradicable weakness of the whole *religionsgeschichtliche* school.

(2) *Existential Philosophy.* Another important influence upon Bultmann which has affected his approach to the history of Jesus has been the philosophy of Heidegger. It is Bultmann's conviction that an existential encounter with Christ is of paramount importance in Christian faith, and this led him to play down the historical Jesus. Even though little of the true history of Jesus is available, this existential encounter can take place. Such a presupposition naturally conditioned Bultmann in his estimation of the gospel material. There is no doubt that his purpose was to make that material relevant to his contemporaries and this led him to exclude anything which to his mind belonged to the first century, but was irrelevant or unacceptable to the twentieth.

b. *Some Basic Assumptions*

Bultmann, in the treatment of his sources, proceeded on the assumption that there are definite laws governing popular narrative and tradition. He first supposed that narratives in course of oral transmission tend to become more explicit and to acquire details lacking in the most primitive form. For example, Luke's mention of the high priest's servant's right ear which was struck off is said to show a development from Mark's account (Luke 22:50; Mark 14:47). Does it necessarily follow that more detailed accounts must be less primitive? Could not both the detailed and the less detailed accounts be equally authentic? Bultmann does not consider such a possibility. Moreover, he appeals to apocryphal tradition for the tendency to attach names to people who were unnamed in earlier tradition. Hence Bultmann begins by being skeptical about the names used in the records (cf. Luke 22:8 where the disciples referred to in Mark 14:13 are named as Peter and John). Furthermore, there is said to be a tendency for indirect discourses to become direct discourses (cf. Mark 8:32; Matt. 16:22). That it has happened in some cases that the material is preserved in both forms cannot be denied, but to deduce from this a general law of tradition may be considerably wide of the mark. An alternative explanation might be that the more direct form was nevertheless from an authentic source.

c. *Classification of Materials for the Life of Jesus*

(1) *General Comments.* A brief reference to Bultmann's classifications will not be amiss. (For full details see his *The History of the Synoptic Tradition* [Eng. tr. 1962]). The miracle stories are at once suspect. Sufficient parallels can be cited from pagan sources to show, in Bultmann's opinion, that the gospel miracles conform to a similar pattern. Parallels of forms do not prove similarity of origin. The uniqueness of the gospel stories rests not in their form but in the uniqueness of the miracle worker. Another of Bultmann's forms are apothegms, important sayings of Jesus for which short scenes serve as a framework. He takes the view that the saying may be authentic, while the setting is the creation of the community, although in some cases both are non-authentic. His criterion of differentiation seems to be that what can be conceived as a community product must have been a community product. Clearly this does not follow. The probability of communities creating narratives and sayings is open to most serious challenge. The assumption appears to be that Christian groups would wish to attribute sayings to Jesus which had no basis in fact, because they were the kind of words which the Christ of faith might be expected to say. Of the biographical apothegms (e.g., as the calling of the disciples in Mark 1:16-20) Bultmann maintains that they give expression "to what Christians had experienced of their Master or what he had experienced at the hands of his people." They become therefore symbols instead of historical events.

It is difficult to believe that any Christian author would have written what purports to be a historical narrative if his intentions were purely symbolical. Nor is it much easier to conceive that the evangelists genuinely thought that the materials used were historical, even if much of it was the symbolic creation of some community or other. Where can parallels be found for such a procedure? The apocryphal literature, which abounds in narratives regarding Jesus and the apostles, which are manifestly the creations of the apocryphal authors, cannot furnish an adequate parallel, for these are stamped so evidently with fantasy that no contemporary ever placed them on the same footing as the canonical Gospels. Moreover, the majority of these productions were written in the interests of some aberration from Christian doctrine. They are too late to provide any guide to the probable procedure of the primitive Church.

(2) *Methods of Dealing With the Words of Jesus.* When Bultmann deals with the sayings of Jesus, he assumes, to begin with, that some are authentic and some are not. This leads him to seek some method of distinguishing between them. He first maintains that different evangelists have placed the same saying in different contexts, which means that one cannot now know what the original context was. Since the context affects the interpretation, he concludes that one cannot now know the meaning as it was originally intended. For example, the sayings about salt and light in Matthew 5:13-15; Mark 4:21; 9:50; Luke 11:33; 14:34, 35, are compared, and the conclusion is reached that each evangelist is experimenting with his interpretations. This principle is then applied generally even to sayings which occur in only one gospel, e.g., many of the parables. In the case of the parables, Bultmann also appeals to rabbinic parallels. An example of his method in reconstructing the words of Jesus is seen in his treatment of the Son of Man saying in Matthew 10:32, 33; Mark 8:38; Luke 12:8, 9. Since he considers that it was axiomatic for the Christian community that Jesus was the Son of man, he maintains that this belief has affected the original saying which drew a distinction between them. Bultmann does not explain how it became axiomatic for the church, if it was not derived from Jesus Himself.

He is not content to suggest modification of Jesus' words. He considers that frequently words spoken by other Jewish teachers or words first used in the Christian community were put into the mouth of Christ. As examples he cites some of the wisdom words of Jesus which can be paralleled from Jewish sources (cf. Luke 12:16-20 and Sirach 11:18, 19). His basic assumption is that parallels point to non-authenticity. When dealing with the prophetic and apocalyptic sayings, he is rather more inclined to find some authentic sayings, since the eschatological enthusiasm of the early Christians was probably derived from the prophetic appearance of Jesus.

Another of Bultmann's categories is Law sayings. Of these he says, "Even though many of the sayings may have originated in the community, the spirit that lives in them goes back to the work of Jesus" (*Form Criticism,* [Eng. tr. 1934], 58). The reason for this greater willingness to accept these Law sayings is their fundamental disagreement with contemporary Judaism. Sayings supported by Old Testament citations and those containing rules of discipline are suspect as community products. Sometimes Bultmann expresses his views as possibilities, but more often he makes statements dogmatically, as when he maintains that the passion predictions in Mark (8:31; 9:31; 10:33, 34) "were first created by the Christian community" (*op. cit.,* 59).

From the above it might be supposed that Bultmann is skeptical about all the sayings of Jesus, but he does attach historical credence to some, as the following extract shows. "Though one may admit the fact that for no single word of Jesus is it possible to produce positive evidence of its authenticity, still one may point to a whole series of words found in the oldest stratum of tradition which do give a consistent representation of the historical message of Jesus" (*op. cit.,* 61). Such are sayings which echo the prophetic calls to repentance, those which announce salvation and those which express the consciousness of the prophet. Bultmann lays great stress on the prophetic role of Jesus.

(3) *The Idea of Legends.* Another category to which he appeals is legend, which, in his view, became attached to the narratives through cultic influences. Such legends would serve the needs of the worshiping community. This applies to the passion narrative (e.g., the death of Judas and the watch at the tomb), the resurrection narrative ("composed in the interests of faith and under the influence of devout imagination"), the Supper (which was referred back to the last meal of Jesus and was transformed into a cult legend), the baptismal narrative, the Transfiguration, the Temptation, the entry into Jerusalem, and many other narratives. When all the overgrowth of legend which Bultmann finds in the sources is removed, it will be seen

that there is little left which can be considered historical. This is why he disputes the possibility of knowledge of the historical Jesus. All he will allow is some knowledge of His message, which he sums up as two-fold: eschatological and ethical, both understood existentially.

From this survey of Bultmann's position it will be apparent that his view of the sources of the life of Jesus is radically different from the traditional view of the Christian Church. Although it may be a matter of indifference to Bultmann, whether or not the historical Jesus can be traced and known, such indifference is not characteristic of New Testament scholars generally, and even among Bultmann's closest disciples is being questioned to some extent. The emergence of a reaction within the Bultmann school is significant because it reflects dissatisfaction with his outright skepticism.

5. *The New Quest*

The reaction has become known as "The New Quest of the Historical Jesus." This description must be understood against the background of the older liberal quest, although its advocates vigorously reject the liberal Jesus. What they are concerned to do is in some measure to fill the gap between the Jesus of history and the Christ of faith. E. Kasemann (cf. his *Essays on New Testament Themes* [Eng. tr. 1960]) has done this by fastening attention on the preaching of Jesus. By this means he hoped to avoid the risk of Docetism (which drew a distinction between the human Jesus and the divine Christ and which concentrated on the latter at the expense of the former) and to bridge the gap between the earthly Jesus and the Church's proclamation of faith. Kasemann recognized, as Bultmann did not, the authority of Jesus as a preacher and as an exorciser of demons.

G. Bornkamm (*Jesus of Nazareth* [Eng. tr. 1960]) goes further and includes aspects of Jesus' attitude toward people (as, for instance, His readiness to forgive sins). In this case the records have preserved certain aspects of the historical Jesus.

Another "New Quester" is E. Fuchs (*Studies of the Historical Jesus* [Eng. tr. 1960]) whose main interest in the historical Jesus is in His determination to minister to social outcasts, like tax collectors and sinners. This is His mission and by it He reveals God's will. His attitude to His death has been influenced by the death of John the Baptist. E. Fuchs departs from the Bultmann position by asserting some continuity between the proclamation of Jesus and the *kerygma*, and by focusing on some psychological aspects which Bultmann neglected.

J. M. Robinson (*The Problem of History in Mark* [1957]) maintains a closer relationship between the historical Jesus in the gospels and the kerygmatic Christ, to such an extent that he has been charged with reversion to the liberal quest, but he has defended his position by claiming that his quest is centered on the existential selfhood and not the personality of Jesus (*A New Quest of the Historical Jesus* [1959]). The difference in terminology may be noted, but Robinson's critics are not convinced that he means anything different.

Throughout the debate which has developed among his own supporters, Bultmann has consistently denied any essential relationship between the historic Jesus and the kerygmatic Christ. His point is not so much the impossibility as the irrelevance of such a connection.

Before any effective use can be made of the gospel records in a presentation of the events in the life of Jesus, the interpreter must make clear his own position in regard to the influence of the *kerygma.* It cannot be assumed that the apostolic *kerygma* bore no relation to the proclamation of Jesus Himself. There is no proof for this, and in the absence of proof the interpreter has every right to assume that the evangelists have presented material which they believed to be historical. Since the church accepted the records without question, all in it must equally have believed in the historicity of the events recorded. In the presence of a considerable number of eyewitnesses it is inconceivable that material which had no foundation in fact could have been created by communities. The Christ of faith becomes unintelligible apart from continuity with the historical Jesus.

6. *The Redaktionsgeschichte School*

This movement has arisen out of form criticism and concentrates on the edited forms of the material; i.e., it treats the gospels rather than the units, although the units are presupposed. The evangelists are viewed as theologians who have imparted something of their own ideas to the material. In some respects this movement is derived from Wrede's approach to Mark's gospel. The difference is that whereas Wrede began with presuppositions regarding the Messianic secret, modern interpreters are more inclined to begin with the gospel material and work back to the writer's theology. There is no doubt that concentration upon the importance of the evangelists is all to the good, for during the period of form criticism this had been largely overlooked. The question arises whether accounts written by authors with a specific theological approach could be considered valid sources for the life of Jesus. None of the evangelists were free from theological influences. They were all personally involved with the Christian faith. They were conscious that the Jesus they were describing in their gospels was more to them at the time of writing than He was to His contemporaries at the time of the events recorded. But it is not true to say that Mark has theologized the history. His record gives the impression of a deep interest in the facts (cf. C. F. D. Moule, "The Intention of the Evangelists," *New Testament Essays,* ed. A. J. B. Higgins [1959]).

It is Bornkamm who has specially drawn attention to Matthew's theological interests. He deals with Matthew's Christology, ecclesiology, and eschatology (in *Tradition and Interpretation in Matthew,* with G. Barth and H. Held, [Eng. tr. 1963]). Under the first, Jesus is presented as Israel's humiliated king and then, after the resurrection, as a world-wide teacher. Under the second, the focus is upon the application of the Mosaic Law to the new community; and under the third, upon the period of the mission of the community. A similar position is taken by G. Barth and H. Held. It is assumed that tradition and interpretation have been interwoven.

The gospel of Luke presents a different phenomenon. Hans Conzelmann (*The Theology of Luke,* [Eng. tr. 1960] attributes a great deal to Luke's theological interests and correspondingly discounts him as an historian. He approaches the gospel from the standpoint of Luke's threefold time scheme – the time of Israel, the time of Jesus, and the time of the church. The gospel is concerned, therefore, with the middle of time. In addition to gearing his interpretation to this point of view, Conzelmann sees much more importance in Luke's geographical references than had previously been the case, attaching to them a symbolic significance, particularly Jerusalem. Clearly the challenge of these various theories must be faced. If the evangelists were primarily theologians, could they have produced history? There seems to be no reason why not, although their purpose was at no time a bare recital of facts, but an endeavor to present the object of their faith in an enduring light.

7. *The Heilsgeschichte Movement*

This trend places emphasis upon the acts of God in history. The historical Jesus becomes a vital part of the revelation of God. Some who follow this movement are nearer to a conservative position than others. The nearest is perhaps Oscar Cullmann, who insists that no true Christian faith can exist apart from a belief that Jesus conceived Himself to be the Messiah (*Christology of the New Testament*, 2nd. ed. [1963]). To Him, revelation resides not only in the interpretation but in the event itself. Because of this he attaches importance to eyewitnesses. In these aspects he is diametrically opposed to the views of the more radical form critics. He has done much to redress the balance in showing the importance of history in the *kerygma*.

The foregoing survey has been necessary before outlining the sources because of the wide variety of opinions concerning them. The debate will go on, but there is no reason to withhold from the attempt to survey the data which have come down from the first century for assessing the life of Christ.

4

Literary Sources for the Life of Christ

In any historical reconstruction, sources of information are indispensable, and these have never been more important than in the account of the historical Jesus. All the available sources will now be collated.

A. The Synoptic Gospels

1. *The Synoptic Problem*

The reason why Matthew, Mark and Luke are known as synoptic gospels is that they follow a common pattern in describing the ministry of Jesus. What is known as the synoptic problem arises when these three gospels are compared with one another. Both the similarities and the differences are significant. Sometimes there are three witnesses to the same incident, sometimes two, and not infrequently only one. In many cases the witnesses agree verbally, in other cases they do not. Two major questions arise: in what order did the gospels originate, and what is their precise relationship to each other?

It will not be necessary here to go into detail over the various solutions of this problem, but some indication must be given, since the approach to the literary sources will inevitably influence the approach to the historical Jesus. The traditional view of gospel origins was that Matthew was the prior gospel and that Mark was no more than an extract from Matthew. This was Augustine's view and held sway until well into the nineteenth century. Of the three gospels, Matthew was the most used. This view tended to cause Mark to fall into neglect as a source of data for the historical Jesus. It is still maintained by some Roman Catholic scholars (e.g., C. Butler, L. Vaganay, and L.

Cerfaux) that Matthew is prior, but with considerable modifications of the older traditional form of the theory.

2. *The Priority of Mark*

Both the other synoptic gospels have been regarded as prior by various scholars. Whereas few have supported the priority of Luke, most modern scholars have concluded for the priority of Mark as offering the best solution to this difficult problem. It cannot even now be considered as an unchallengeable hypothesis, nor must its hypothetical character be forgotten. Acceptance of the Markan hypothesis draws attention to one important aspect of the historical data. It was strongly attested in the ancient tradition that Mark was Peter's interpreter, and if the tradition is true it has obvious bearing on the relation of Mark's gospel to the events recorded. If an eyewitness is behind a writing, it is at once invested with greater importance as a historical source. This would be particularly true of Mark's gospel, as Peter could have been present at most of the events which Mark describes. This traditional ascription has been severely challenged by form critical schools of thought, which deny eyewitness control of the transmitted material. The strength of the external evidence for this tradition cannot be denied and full weight must be given to it. The most important witness is Papias, who claimed that Mark wrote down what he learned from Peter's preaching and that he aimed for accuracy, but was not concerned about order. This means that Papias was not prepared to attach too much importance to Mark's chronology, but did not dispute the historical veracity of his account. Since later patristic writers accept this opinion of Papias regarding Mark's relation to Peter, it must have been considered reliable tradition.

3. *The Sayings Source (Q)*

If this theory of Markan priority is accepted as a beginning point in surveying the materials for a life of Christ, it leads to the problem of the source of the non-Markan material in Matthew and Luke. Mark has a limited scope, consisting mainly of events, and including little teaching material. What then is the main source for the teaching material in Matthew and Luke? The answer generally given is that they were indebted to a common source called "Q," or "Quelle." For the present purpose, "Q," whether it be treated as a written source or as a

symbol for common teaching material, will be restricted to that material which is shared by Matthew and Luke but is not found in Mark. Since this consists almost wholly of sayings of Jesus, it is clearly a most valuable additional source of information about the Jesus of history. Had Mark been the sole source, there would have been little idea of the wide range and variety of the teaching of Jesus, with a consequent lessening of the concept of Him as a teacher. Many source critics therefore place the sayings source on a level with Mark as an important witness to the life of Jesus, but there is an important difference. The existence of Mark as a source is beyond doubt, but the same cannot be said for "Q." There is no external evidence, as there is for Mark, concerning the one who produced it, nor is there any indication of the source of the material contained in it. Did it have apostolic sanction? Was it based on witnesses? Can it be assumed that care was taken to preserve the sayings of Jesus without corruption? Since the "Q" source is generally considered to be the major source for this teaching material, some answers to these questions are clearly of basic importance.

Some have supposed that Matthew was its author, on the strength of what Papias said about Matthew writing the "Oracles" (of Jesus). If this is a true deduction from Papias, it would supply apostolic authority for the sayings collection. Matthew must have heard Jesus teach many times and may well have been present on most of the occasions when discourses or connected sayings are attributed to Him. But this interpretation of Papias' words was probably not Irenaeus' understanding of them, for he repeated similar wording but makes Matthew the author of an Aramaic gospel. This was the common conviction of the ancients. If Matthew was not the author of "Q," who was? There is no satisfactory answer. If such a source existed, all that can be asserted is that it was clearly highly regarded by both Matthew and Luke for them both to incorporate it in their gospels.

While the possibility of a sayings collection cannot be denied, its hypothetical character has caused some scholars to look elsewhere for a solution. The view that Matthew used Luke, although not without difficulties, would at once dispense with "Q" (as A. M. Farrer has pointed out, "On Dispensing with 'Q'," *Studies in the Gospels*, ed. D. E. Nineham [1955]). This would enhance the value of Matthew as a source, for it would mean that the sayings material incorporated by him was the result of his

own collection, if the apostolic authorship is maintained. Whoever is the author of the first gospel, the strong patristic connection of the gospel with Matthew's name shows the high esteem in which all the material, including the teaching portion, was held. To maintain a close contact between Matthew and the sayings material is, therefore, not only more in harmony with the external evidence, but is also more satisfactory than attributing "Q" to an anonymous author.

4. *Material Peculiar to Matthew and Luke*

Following up the "Q" hypothesis, attention must be drawn to the material peculiar to Matthew and Luke. These two authors record considerably more material separately than is recorded by Mark alone. There has been a tendency among many scholars to prefer what appears in two or three witnesses as superior to what is testified to by only one. A single witness cannot for that reason alone be considered suspect. Such a principle of criticism would at once put Matthew's and Luke's special material at a discount, but this is not historically sound. The reliability of a witness depends on the reliability of his character and not on the existence or otherwise of other witnesses to corroborate what he says. Nonetheless, some of Matthew's special material has been regarded as less authentic because it raises difficult apologetic problems. Such details as John the Baptist's hesitation to baptize Jesus, the coin found in the fish's mouth, and the opening of the graves during the crucifixion are considered secondary tradition because of the difficulties which they raise.

That there is need for explanation is undeniable, but that the material must be considered secondary through ecclesiastical influence upon the tradition is not self-evident. The heightening of the miraculous is of such a character that it is difficult to imagine that it would have remained unchallenged had it been wholly fictitious. In any case, the proportion of material in this category is so small a part of the whole of Matthew's special material that it would be unjustifiable if it were allowed to dominate any evaluation of the whole.

Both Matthew and Luke include special sections dealing with the sayings of Jesus. Matthew generally combines his with the material assigned to "Q," whereas Luke is more inclined to keep his separate. Both include parables of Jesus, but their differences are significant. Matthew's are generally Kingdom parables, whereas Luke's are not so specified. Moreover, Luke's parables tend to concentrate on a more personal interest than Matthew's. This difference reveals the individual approach of the two evangelists, and also points to the wide variety of the teaching material of Jesus. Comparison of the matter peculiar to each with that common to both reveals the additional insights which their individual choice of sayings provides.

For instance, the Sermon on the Mount in Matthew contains considerably more sayings than Luke's Sermon on the Plain, particularly about Jesus' attitude toward the Law. Similarly, our knowledge of many incidents and sayings from the latter part of the Lord's ministry is wholly dependent upon Luke (e.g., Zacchaeus, the parables of the lost things). Some comment will be made later on the particular contribution of each evangelist toward a reconstruction of the historical Jesus, but now the purpose is to draw attention to the value of sources of information which are peculiar to any of them. Unless there is some adequate reason for regarding such sources as inferior, it is reasonable to receive them as data for a historical reconstruction.

5. *The Birth Narratives*

One special aspect of both Matthew and Luke is their inclusion of birth narratives which are clearly drawn from entirely different sources. It has rightly been pointed out that Matthew shows more clearly Joseph's position, whereas Luke's narratives are more concerned with Mary's. Some scholars have contended that in both accounts the narratives have been influenced by Old Testament motives, but there is a difference between narratives created from Old Testament patterns and those influenced by Old Testament thought. Matthew includes many instances in his birth narratives of fulfillments of Old Testament prophecy, but any suggestion that he has created the narratives to fit in with the prediction is unworthy of the high spiritual tone of these narratives as a whole.

Some have seen in Luke's narratives something in the nature of a poetic idyll which was never intended to be regarded as historical, but if this is so it is strange that Luke takes such pains to stress that his gospel was based on careful historical inquiry (Luke 1:1-4). It is reasonable to suppose that Luke received the material for his birth narratives from a reliable source. There is, in fact, no reason why he should not have had communication with Mary, although this cannot be proved. Some prefer to maintain that Luke has incorporated into his gospel an earlier source which dealt with the birth story.

Some mention must be made of the theory that Matthew used a book of Old Testament testimonies to Jesus, if only to point out the great importance of the idea of fulfillment in the gospel accounts. Matthew includes twelve citations introduced by a special formula apparently drawn from the Hebrew rather than the LXX, and this has given rise to the theory that he used a testimony book containing Old Testament citations which had a bearing on the events in the life of Jesus the Messiah. A modification of this theory is that the early church was more interested in passages which contained Messianic predictions than in isolated Old Testament texts bearing on the life of the Messiah (cf. C. H. Dodd, *According to the Scriptures* [1952]). Whether either of these theories, or alternatively the further suggestion that the collection is the work of the evangelist is true, is immaterial for the present purpose. What is important is that none of the synoptic gospels, or for that matter the fourth gospel either, treats the events and teaching of Jesus in isolation from the Old Testament. His incarnation, ministry, death, and resurrection were all viewed by the early Christians as fulfillments of Old Testament predictions. No approach to the life of Jesus is valid which does not give considerable weight to the Old Testament background.

B. The Fourth Gospel

1. *The Problems of Historicity*

The use of this gospel as a source of data for the life of Jesus has been variously regarded throughout the period of New Testament criticism. Sometimes the synoptics have been regarded as superior, and sometimes John has held first place. Throughout the first half of the twentieth century John's gospel was discounted as a historical source, but there has latterly been a greater readiness to reinstate it. This has been due in no small measure to the discovery of the Dead Sea Scrolls. It would be a mistake to maintain that the connection between these scrolls and John's gospel was close, but what parallels there are support the view that both may belong to a similar milieu of thought. This means that the gospel cannot be considered a wholly Hellenistic production in which the author attempts to present a Hellenistic portrait of Jesus, as earlier scholars had frequently maintained, but must be viewed against the background of a Jewish syncretistic milieu. If the men of Qumran could talk in abstract terms (e.g. the symbolic use of light and darkness), there is no reason why Jesus should not have done the same. It is against such a "new look" on the fourth gospel (to use Bishop J. A. T. Robinson's phrase (*Twelve New Testament Studies* [1962]), that the Johannine problem must be considered in its bearing on the historical Jesus.

The first consideration is to decide what relation the gospel has to the events which it relates. Did the writer intend to write facts, or interpretation, or both? In what sense can the details of the narratives be considered historically valid? No answer to these questions can begin in a better place than with John's purpose, according to his own statement (John 20:30, 31). Whereas he makes clear his evangelistic purpose – to lead to faith in Jesus as the Christ and as Son of God – yet the faith is based on "signs" which have been performed in the presence of the disciples. The basic facts of the gospel were therefore verifiable by responsible witnesses. It cannot be denied that what John purports to write has a close connection with events that happened, although his own purpose is concerned with the Christ of faith. In view of John's stated purpose, the theological aspect of his gospel must be borne in mind throughout. He was not concerned to write bare history, but history with a specific aim in view.

The validity of the history will naturally depend on the trustworthiness of the author, and this raises the whole problem of authorship. It is not my intention to discuss the problem here, but rather to consider the effects of various suggestions on the problem of historicity. If the traditional view that the apostle John is the author be maintained, the validity of the data must be highly ranked, for the whole gospel would then be basically an eyewitness account. Much more importance would attach to the farewell discourses (John 13-17) if the author had been personally present. In spite of the external evidence, corroborated by several internal hints of an eyewitness, many have found difficulty with this view and have postulated another author – either a John the Elder or else some entirely anonymous person. Most who dispute apostolic authorship, however, do concede some apostolic connection (except many Continental scholars).

Some regard the apostle John as the witness behind the gospel, if he is not the author.

The problem of authorship is less crucial than that of history. A few illustrations will show the force of this. In the realm of chronology John places a cleansing of the Temple near the beginning of the ministry of Jesus, whereas the synoptists place it at the end. If John's narrative is taken symbolically of the cleansing of Judaism by Jesus, the chronological problem ceases to exist. But the record does not read like a symbolic account. Another problem is the form of teaching. The absence of parables and the presence of much discourse material, including rabbinic type dialogue, marks John off from the synoptic gospels. The problem is not insuperable, for some parabolic forms are included in John in addition to the allegories of the Vine and Shepherd, while some extended discourse material is found in the other gospels, particularly Matthew. Moreover, it must be remembered that John's material almost wholly centers in Jerusalem, whereas the synoptists concentrate on Galilee. In spite of the historical difficulties, it is not impossible to integrate John as a historical source with the synoptic gospels.

2. *The Relationship to the Synoptic Gospels*

A comparison of John with the synoptics shows how much he has left out and also how much new material he has included. The question naturally arises whether John is independent of the synoptic gospels or whether he used them as a source. In view of the small amount of material common to all the gospels, there is much to be said for the theory that John did not use the others as literary sources. The largest amount of common material is in the Passion narrative. It seems indisputable that John assumed the synoptic tradition even if he did not use them as sources. He speaks, for instance, of the Twelve without further definition. His omission of the institution of the Lord's Supper would be unintelligible if he did not assume that details of this were already widely known. It is a reasonable hypothesis that John intended his gospel to be complementary to the synoptics. There was no question in his mind that his gospel would be used alongside the others. Patristic testimony shows that at a fairly early period this happened. John and the synoptics were the only gospels found acceptable. It must not be overlooked that whatever incongruities modern scholars find between John and the synoptics, the ancients were not conscious of them, with the sole exception of a group known as the Alogi, who were opposed to John's doctrine.

The major problem facing the historian of the life of Jesus is to find some satisfactory way of dovetailing the separate accounts. The cleansing of the Temple is an example. Some decision must be made about this, either the postulation of a double cleansing or else a choice between the Johannine and synoptic chronology. Most choose the synoptic dating, but the former suggestion is not impossible. The dating of the Last Supper is another well-known crux, since John appears to set it on Nisan 13, while the synoptics prefer Nisan 14. Another problem is to fit into the Galilean account of the ministry in the synoptics the events recorded by John as happening at Jerusalem. Moreover, the length of the public ministry of Jesus poses a problem, for John suggests that the period must be at least two if not three years, whereas the synoptics give the impression of one year. The matter is not irresoluble, since a reference to a harvest in the midst of the synoptic ministry shows that more than one year must have been involved, although the events appear on the surface to have happened all within two Passovers. Clearly the synoptists were not as interested in the festival days as John, who for this very reason must be regarded as a better guide in such matters of chronology.

Attempts at harmonizing must at best be regarded as tentative and in some cases as purely arbitrary. In dealing with such sources, one must conclude that the chronological data in the gospels are so sparse that it is impossible to reconstruct the order of events with any certainty. Unless the purpose is to trace some psychological development in the mind of Jesus, the order of events is of little importance. Of the major events there can be no question. The absence of chronological data makes a biography impossible, but the material is sufficient to show the reality of the Jesus of history. In the outline that follows some order had to be selected. In many points of detail the order chosen is admittedly arbitrary.

C. The Fourfold Presentation of Jesus

It is significant that in spite of an early attempt at producing a harmony of the gospels (i.e. by Tatian), it was always preferred to keep the gospels separate. Each presents its own portrait and each is needed for the total picture. It will be valuable, therefore, to give some indication of the characteristic features of each evangelist's presentation of Jesus, for this is more valid than any attempt to reconstruct a continuous account from material in all four gospels.

1. *Matthew's Portrait*

This has many distinctive features. His portrayal is like a royal figure. The line of descent in the genealogy is through David, who is named at the head of the second main section in Matthew's list. The expression "Son of David" occurs on various occasions in the gospel, to a greater extent than in the other synoptics. Matthew's birth narrative concentrates on homage fit for a king (Matthew 2), as compared with Luke's account of the worship of the lowly shepherds. In the narrative of the triumphal entry into Jerusalem, both Matthew and Luke refer to the kingly scene, but only Matthew cites the Old Testament passage, "Behold, your King is coming to you." While all the synoptics mention Jesus' teaching about the Kingdom of God, it is Matthew in particular who concentrates upon it. His parables are Kingdom parables. The message of Jesus is concerned with the proclamation of the Kingdom.

Another characteristic of this gospel is the authoritative nature of Jesus as a teacher. In the great discourses which Matthew has sandwiched between blocks of narrative, he specially emphasizes the teaching ministry of Jesus. Yet, he does not portray Jesus as a Jewish rabbi. In fact, Jesus claims authority to supersede the Law, which the rabbis considered their highest duty to uphold. In view of this fundamental difference, it is no wonder that Jesus so often was at variance with the religious leaders of His day. Matthew comments that "he taught as one who had authority and not as the scribes" (Matthew 7:29; cf. Mark 1:22; Luke 4:32, where similar comment is made about Jesus' visit to the synagogue). Matthew's gospel is dominated by his five great discourse sections – Matthew 5-7; 10; 13; 18; 23-25 – which illustrate various aspects of the teaching of Jesus about the Kingdom.

Matthew shares with the other gospels the picture of Jesus as Son of Man, a title which Jesus uses both redemptively and eschatologically. He also shares with them the belief in the Messianic claims of Jesus. He alone records the words of Jesus about the coming church and gives some indication of its nature (cf. Matt. 16:18 ff.; 18:15 ff.). In this respect this gospel leads into the early church period, for it is Matthew who gives the Great Commission of Jesus to His disciples before His ascension and ends with the assurance of Jesus' continuing presence with them. One cannot put aside this gospel without awareness of the future of the people of God because of the resurrection of Jesus Christ.

2. *Mark's Portrait*

Mark's distinctive contribution is one of emphasis rather than unique material. The first feature is the constant activity of Jesus. The relative absence of teaching material contributes to this impression. Mark often says that the actions of Jesus were performed "immediately." One saying may fittingly be chosen as summing up Mark's portrait of Jesus (Mark 10:45; cf. Matt. 20:28), that the Son of man came not to be served but to serve. His is essentially the gospel of Christ the servant, a gospel full of bustling activity which would make a great appeal to men of action. Jesus was no religious recluse, but a man deeply aware of the needs of those around Him.

This gospel is also remarkable for the large proportion of space devoted to the passion and resurrection narratives. There is little specific teaching about the meaning of Christ's death (except Mark 10:45), but the arrangement of the whole gospel gives the impression that for Mark the real focus was upon the concluding events, and that the opening two-thirds of the gospel was only a preparation for this. Mark obviously did not attempt to write a biography. Indeed, it is he alone of all the evangelists who describes his book as "the gospel of Jesus Christ" (Mark 1:1). Undoubtedly for him the major part of that gospel was the redemptive work accomplished by Jesus on the cross.

It should be noted that Mark begins by identifying Jesus as Son of God (according to the most probable reading) and yet proceeds to include, more than any of the other gospels, a presentation of Jesus as Son of man. Since Mark seems more drawn by actions than by words, it is most natural to see the evidence of both these titles in what Jesus did, rather than what He said. The humanity of Jesus may be seen in His acts of compassion, and His divine power in the fact that so many of these acts of compassion are portrayed as miracles.

Mention has already been made of those who have claimed

that Mark has imposed his own theory of a Messianic secret upon his material, but since the theory is not demanded by the evidence, it may be said that Mark's portrait of Jesus implies the awareness of His own Messianic mission. The earthly life of Jesus was not the appointed time for this to be made known. The Messiah must first be recognized in the risen Christ.

3. *Luke's Portrait*

There is a warm human touch in Luke's account. The birth stories are more intimate. The contacts of Jesus with the people of His day are more varied, with special emphasis upon His concern for women and children. The parables more frequently have a human touch about them, as is specially illustrated in the parables of Luke 15:8 ff. Luke records more of the theme of joy in Jesus' teaching than the other evangelists. The ministry of Jesus was not intended to give a somber impression. Even in his Passion references Luke dwells less on the tragic aspects, although no description of the crucifixion scene can avoid such an aspect. In Luke's account of the transfiguration, the conversation concerned the "exodus" of Jesus rather than His death (Luke 9:31). When he describes the crucifixion scene, he does not include Jesus' cry of separation, "Why hast thou forsaken me," included by both Matthew and Mark. In Luke the last words of Jesus are a prayer of committal to the Father. Nevertheless, if the starkness of the cross is somewhat toned down, its centrality is as clear in Luke as in the others. It is in Luke that the risen Christ is recorded as expounding from the Scriptures the necessity for His sufferings (24:26, 27). He ends his gospel on a note of great joy, which was now no longer dependent upon the earthly presence of Jesus. In no clearer way could Luke have indicated the continuity of the historical Jesus with the Christ of faith.

4. *John's Portrait*

The Johannine portrait is different, although there are many common features with the other gospels which enable the portrait to be identified as the same person. He is introduced in a different way, in the concept of a divine intermediary, the divine Word who nevertheless became flesh. There is nothing comparable in the synoptics. Had John proceeded in the same vein throughout his gospel, the difference in approach would have been insuperable. As soon as John has spoken of the incarnation, his narrative proceeds to illustrate in human terms what it meant for the Word to become flesh.

The most marked characteristic of His portrait is the filial relationship between Jesus and the Father. This is essentially the gospel of Jesus, the Son. Its purpose was that men might believe that Jesus is the Son of God, and the author took care that much of the gospel testifies to this fact. Scattered throughout the gospel are statements which show the consciousness of Jesus and of His dependence on the Father. He is the Sent One. It is the Father's will that He has done. He calls men to the Father's purpose for them. The climax of this aspect of Jesus is seen in the prayer in John 17, which has not inappropriately been called the high priestly prayer, but which is really a filial supplication on behalf of His disciples.

Another feature of John's portrait is the miraculous signs which are included as an attestation of Jesus. These signs are intended to be authenticating and are said to redound to God's glory. The signs are themselves in agreement with the portrait of the divine Son. They are the deeds which the Son might be expected to perform. They were further intended to be aids to faith, for Jesus Himself appealed to His works if men would not believe Him for His own sake.

Linked with these characteristics is the remarkable fact that John records more evidence of the perfect humanity of Jesus than any of the other evangelists. Jesus is described as thirsty and tired. At Lazarus' tomb He is moved with indignation. He does the most menial service in the upper room. There is no doubt about the fact that the Word had become flesh. This Johannine portrait was wholly different from the Docetic representation of Jesus, in which His humanity was more apparent than real.

There is a certain unhurried atmosphere about this gospel, in strong contrast to Mark's. Jesus has time to discuss and converse. The action is slow-moving and sometimes non-existent. There is more sense of inevitability about this portrait than about the others. The idea of the "hour" of destiny runs through the whole gospel. At first it is said that it has not yet come, and this prepares the reader to look for its dawning and draws the narrative to a climax, when eventually it does come in the Passion narrative. There is nothing accidental about the cross; it is seen as part of the purpose of God.

When these four portraits are compared, they present four different aspects of Jesus, none of which can be dispensed with without loss. Any attempt at reconstructing the historical Jesus cannot proceed without recognizing the many-sided character of the person of Jesus as the four evangelists saw Him.

D. Other New Testament Evidence for the Life of Jesus

An important question arises over the relation of the Acts and epistles to the testimony of the gospels to the historical Jesus. The Pauline epistles are of particular interest. One needs to inquire what knowledge these epistles reveal of Paul's acquaintance with the events and the teaching of Jesus. First impressions might suggest that Paul was either ignorant of or else uninterested in the historical Jesus. Such impressions would not be entirely justified, for there are passing allusions in the epistles which bear testimony to his knowledge of certain historical facts.

When Paul is contending with the Judaizers at Galatia, he asserts that "God sent forth his Son, born of woman, born under the Law" (Gal. 4:4), by which it is clear that he regarded Him as a true man who lived in an environment of Jewish Law. According to human reckoning He was of the seed of David (Rom. 1:3). Whether this latter reference is regarded as part of the primitive *kerygma* (as C. H. Dodd believes, *The Apostolic Preaching and its Developments* [2nd ed. 1944]), or as Paul's own thought, is of small consequence. It shows, however, Paul's acquaintance with the lineage of Jesus through the Davidic line.

Some glimpses of his knowledge of the character of Jesus are seen from his references to the meekness and gentleness of Christ (II Cor. 10:1), the compassion of Christ (Phil. 1:8) and his willingness to bear reproaches (Rom. 15:3). Some background knowledge of the historical Jesus would appear to be indispensable if these expressions are to have intelligible meaning for Paul and his readers. The apostle is certainly aware of the external circumstances of the life of Jesus, for he refers to the poverty of Christ in II Corinthians 8:9. Moreover, there are references to Him as an example, and this must presuppose some detailed knowledge of His actions.

It is concerning the passion and resurrection of Jesus that there is the greatest clarity in the testimony of Paul. He knows about the betrayal (I Cor. 11:23). Those who crucified Him are said to be "the rulers of this age" (2:8), although he includes the Jews as partners in the offense (I Thess. 2:14, 15). His knowledge of the resurrection is detailed (I Cor. 15:3 ff.). This passage repays careful attention, for it supplies information additional to the gospel accounts. The death and burial of Jesus are mentioned before the resurrection appearances to show the connection of these appearances with the historical events. Since Paul states explicitly that he had "received" this information, it is evident that no small importance was attached in the primitive period to the fact of the burial. Of special interest is the mention of the appearances. To begin with, some of the gospel appearances are omitted, e.g., the appearance to the women and to the two on the Emmaus road. Whether the five hundred refers to the same people to whom Luke refers (Luke 24:50) on the occasion when Jesus ascended is not clear, but only Paul mentions the number. Moreover, it is he alone who refers to an appearance to James. It is not easy to fit in Paul's data with those mentioned in the gospels, but for that reason the evidence must be regarded as independent. The primitive *kerygma* clearly emphasized the need for historical verification of the central factor of the Christian faith. The resurrection was certainly more than a subjective experience.

Paul is specific about the details of the institution of the Last Supper, but his account supplements the gospel records by preserving the Lord's words, "Do this as often as you drink it, in remembrance of me" (I Cor. 11:25). This section is of particular interest, as Paul maintains that he received the tradition from the Lord, by which he must mean that the tradition carried with it the divine sanction.

There are various occasions when Paul appears to be referring to the teaching of Jesus in a way which shows his acquaintance with it. It is possible that his reference to love as a fulfillment of the Law (Rom. 13:10; Gal. 5:14) is an echo of the teaching of Jesus. More specific is the occasion when Paul, on the issue of marriage, distinguishes between his own opinion and the express teaching of Jesus, although he clearly believed that his opinion was in harmony with that teaching (I Cor. 7:10-12, 25). In the pastoral epistles two references may be noted. Timothy is advised that true teachers must conform their teaching to "the sound words of our Lord Jesus Christ" (I Tim. 6:3), which could be a reference to words taught by Him. The other reference is linked with a Scriptural citation

(I Tim. 5:18) which is clearly a saying of Jesus, and possibly a quotation (Luke 10:7), to the effect that the laborer deserves his wages.

Some have found difficulty in the fact that Paul does not show more acquaintance with the historic facts of the life of Jesus. This is not altogether unexpected. The epistles are incidental correspondence dealing with practical and theological problems which arose in the church. The fact is that there are few occasions within the epistles where recording of events and sayings of Jesus would have been appropriate. But it may be said that the epistles are written against such a basic understanding of the historical Jesus that they would not have been intelligible without it. (Cf. R. J. Knowling's *Witness of the Epistles* [1892] and his *Testimony of St. Paul to Christ* [1905]).

The witness of the book of Acts shows everywhere an emphasis on the death and resurrection of Jesus as the major content of the early preaching. What information does it supply about the life of Jesus? The most obvious is the brief résumé in Peter's address to Cornelius and his household (Acts 10:36 ff.). Peter speaks of Jesus of Nazareth as one anointed by God with the Holy Spirit. His deeds are referred to as doing good and healing (especially exorcisms). Death by hanging on a tree is also mentioned. This testifies to the place of historical details about Jesus in the earlier proclamations. In the earlier speeches there is recognition that the responsibility for the crucifixion must rest upon the Jews (cf. Acts 2:23, 36; 7:52) and of the choice of a murderer in place of Jesus (3:14). Both Peter (3:14) and Stephen (7:52) describe Jesus as the Righteous One, thus bearing witness to their knowledge of His holy character.

In the other epistles the data are sparse. In the epistle to the Hebrews there is a knowledge of the Temptation (Heb. 2:18; 4:15). The powerful intercessions of Jesus with strong crying and tears in the days of His flesh are mentioned in Hebrews 5:7, and this seems to be a specific reference to the agony in Gethsemane. There is also a passing allusion to the hostility which Jesus endured (12:3) and which is regarded as an example for the readers. It is clear, therefore, that the writer is conscious of much of the background of the historical Jesus.

In the epistle of James the main feature of interest is the manner in which James so frequently reflects knowledge of the sayings of Jesus, particularly from the Sermon on the Mount (cf.

James 1:2 and Matt. 5:10-12; 1:22 and 7:24 ff.; 5:2 f. and 6:19, to cite only a few examples). This is of particular importance because James reflects more of the sayings of Jesus than any other New Testament author. But James' epistle is the most practical of any, and the ethical teaching of Jesus was for him of greatest relevance.

The Petrine epistles provide a few allusions to the historical Jesus. The suffering of Christ is referred to as an example (I Pet. 2:21) and His sufferings are described (cf. Isa. 53). The statement in I Peter 2:12 about men seeing one's good deeds seems to be an echo of the saying of Jesus in Matthew 5:16. This epistle also preserves the enigmatic statement about Christ preaching to the spirits in prison (I Pet. 3:19), which is nowhere hinted at in the gospels. There is a reference to the Transfiguration of Jesus and to the fact that there were eyewitnesses of this event (II Pet. 1:17 f.). John speaks of what eyes have seen and hands handled (I John 1:1), but gives no historical details. The book of Revelation is centered so much on the heavenly Christ that no reference is made to events in the life of Jesus, but the Lamb is referred to as slain. One saying which recurs – he who has an ear, let him hear – may well be an echo of the words of Jesus.

To sum up, it will be seen that specific data regarding the historic Jesus outside the gospels in the New Testament are frugal, but that everywhere they are assumed. It is no wonder that the early church placed such store on its gospel sources.

E. Extra-canonical Material for the Life of Jesus

There is little information about the history of Jesus from outside the New Testament, and, most of what there is, is unlikely to be authentic; yet every avenue must be explored. The evidence may be divided into the following categories: 1. Non-Christian; 2. Christian archaeological and patristic sources; 3. Apocryphal gospels; and 4. Gnostic works.

1. *Non-Christian Evidences*

Under this, two sub-divisions will be considered, pagan and Jewish. The pagan evidence may be dealt with quickly, since it is practically non-existent. Tacitus reports about the Christians in the time of Nero's persecutions (A.D. 64) and mentions that Christ was executed in the reign of Tiberius by the procurator Pontius Pilate. Pliny in his letter to the emperor Trajan, concerning the superstition of Christianity, refers to Christ, but only as an object of reviling by those persuaded to apostatize. Another historian, Suetonius, mentions the expulsion from Rome of the Jews who had caused a great tumult under the influence of "Chrestus" (who may well be identified with Christ), but he gives no further evidence about Chrestus.

These are the major pagan witnesses to the historical Jesus. In spite of the rapid spread of the Christian church, the pagan world approached no nearer to it than to call the whole movement a superstition which was accompanied by vile practices. Against such a background the progress of the Christian church is remarkable.

When one turns to Jewish evidences the situation is not too different. Three passages in Josephus' *Antiquities* may be noted. One gives an account of Herod's action in killing John the Baptist, which is of value in support of the validity of the gospel records, although there are different motives stated. Another passage makes specific statements about Jesus, although many have disputed the validity of the passage because no writer before Eusebius (fourth century A.D.) mentions it. It may be genuine, and will accordingly be cited in full: "Now about this time arose Jesus, a wise man, if indeed he should be called a man. For he was a doer of marvellous deeds, a teacher of men who receive the truth with pleasure; and he won over to himself many Jews and many also of the Greek (nation). He was the Christ. And when on the indictment of the principal men among us Pilate had sentenced him to the cross, those who had loved him at the first did not cease; for he appeared to them on the third day alive again, the divine prophets having foretold these and ten thousand other wonderful things concerning him. And even now the tribe of Christians named after him is not extinct." This statement certainly seems rather too sympathetic toward Christianity for Josephus, particularly the reference to the resurrection. If it be considered authentic, it shows the extent to which knowledge of the historical Jesus had penetrated into the circle in which this Jewish historian moved. What details are given are in full agreement with the gospel narratives. The third passage in the *Antiquities* mentions Jesus but only insofar as referring to His connection with James, the brother of Jesus, whose murder by the Sanhedrin Josephus describes.

Space will not allow discussion of the passages in the Slavonic version of Josephus' *Jewish War,* for there is considerable doubt about their genuineness as a first century testimony. If any historical value may be attached to them, they witness to the view that Jesus was concerned about armed political agitation.

In addition to the witness of Josephus, Jewish testimony must include references in the Talmud. These references are not numerous and may be restricted to eight, which can be considered of any value. One refers to the hanging of Yeshu of Nazareth and mentions His practice of sorcery. This appears to be a Jewish attempt to explain away the responsibility of the Jews for the crucifixion. The second refers to five disciples of Jesus by name, but none of the names coincide with those mentioned in the gospels. The third describes a proselyte calling up the spirit of Jesus by spells; while the fourth refers to a man "born of a woman" who was to arise and "make himself God," against whom people are warned. There is also a reference to Him departing and coming again. Another feature is the recognition that this man will lead the whole world astray, showing the universal appeal of Christianity. In two sayings there is a description of Jesus (under a pseudonym) as a bastard, reflecting Jewish ridicule of the Virgin Birth. The seventh reference is a saying attributed to Jesus concerning the hire of a harlot, which is almost certainly of doubtful validity; the eighth contains a story involving a Christian philosopher in which reference is made to the Gospel, but the first supposed citation, "Son and daughter shall inherit together," does not occur, neither does the second citation, although it looks like a modified version of Matthew 5:17. (For a concise account of these sayings, cf. R. Dunkerly, *Beyond the Gospels* [1957]). What value is to be placed on these Jewish comments on Jesus must remain doubtful, but the references demonstrate some knowledge of Jesus as a historical figure and give some indication of the scorn with which the Rabbis regarded Him.

2. *Christian Evidences*

During the earliest period of church history extra-canonical evidence is sparse. The present concern will be with two lines of evidence, archaeological and patristic.

In the archaeological field almost the only evidence comes from the catacomb inscriptions. These supply information concerning what the early Christians thought about Jesus rather than information of a historical character. There is an early painting of

Him as a youthful and beardless person, but there is no knowing whether this was based on anyone other than in the imagination of the artist.

There might be some slight contribution from the well-known ROTAS-SATOR word square, which was widely used in early Christian circles. There is considerable dispute over its significance, but it has been suggested that the center word TENET in both directions forms the symbol of a cross, thus reminding the Christians of the basic belief in their faith. Others have seen the square as an indirect reference to the Lord's Prayer in Latin, since the letters in the square make up PATER-NOSTER twice with two A's and two O's surplus, representing Christ as Alpha and Omega. Such evidence is so tenuous that it can contribute nothing to the understanding of the history of Jesus. The same may be said of the famous fish symbol, which testifies to early Christian faith in Christ as Savior.

Among the Apostolic Fathers there are various sayings attributed to Jesus, but the majority of these are variants of canonical sayings, which may well be accounted for by loose reminiscences of the teaching. Clement of Rome has passages of this kind, but it seems best to regard these as evidence of the knowledge by Clement of the canonical sources, rather than as independent evidence. In the *Didaché* there are a number of statements which echo the teaching of Jesus in the Sermon on the Mount, without attributing the words to Jesus. Some think that a genuine saying is recorded by the *Epistle of Barnabas* in the following words, "So he says, Those who wish to see me and lay hold of my kingdom must receive me through tribulation and suffering." While this might be conceived as a genuine saying, it might equally well be no more than a general summary of the gist of Jesus' teaching about those who seek the kingdom. Many canonical sayings mention the tribulation which followers of Jesus must endure.

In the *Epistles of Ignatius* there occurs a resurrection account which differs from the canonical accounts. The *Shepherd of Hermas* is interesting because it includes authoritative parables which are quite different from the canonical gospels, but these are not directly attributed to Jesus. It is extraordinary how little material from the Apostolic Fathers preserves what might conceivably be regarded as genuine non-canonical sayings. It must be noted that not a great many canonical sayings were cited either, but if a large number of "agrapha" (unwritten sayings) were circulating in the oral tradition, it might have been supposed that far more would have been preserved by the earliest writers had they considered them genuine. This kind of argument has obvious limitations, since the purpose of these patristic writers was not focused on showing their acquaintance with the sayings of Jesus.

There is little evidence for one's purpose in the writings of the Apologists, although two testimonies may be mentioned. The *Apology* of Aristides contains passages which show affinity with the gospels, although introducing variations. It is clear that the author is echoing their language without making direct reference to the sayings of Jesus. There is certainly no evidence of non-canonical sayings of Jesus. The other witness is Justin Martyr who mentions the birth of Jesus as having taken place in a cave, in place of the synoptic's stable. Both terms might in this case be correct since stables in caves were not unknown in the East. There are sundry sayings of Jesus which are reminiscent of the gospel sayings. Bearing in mind that Justin is not an accurate quoter it may reasonably be supposed that he himself is responsible for the variations and is not citing some independent traditions. For instance, when Justin records the saying, "I came not to call the righteous to repentance but sinners, for the Heavenly Father desireth the sinner's repentance rather than his punishment," this looks like a Justinian enlargement of Luke 5:32. One of the best attested *agrapha* in Justin is, "In whatsoever things I apprehend you, in these I shall judge you," which is reminiscent of various statements of Jesus on judgment in the gospels, but it may be an independent saying.

3. *Apocryphal Gospels*

A large number of these appeared from the second century onward, and in them are included many incidents which relate either to the birth and childhood of Jesus or to His Passion. None of the material has any claim to be genuine. The additional data are generally fantastic, e.g., the story of Jesus making clay birds which flew away. Moreover, these gospels were generally, if not always, heretical in purpose. The *Gospel of Peter,* for instance, is known to have been published in the interests of the Docetic heresy, for Serapion testified to this fact. It was not difficult for those gripped by a dogmatic purpose of a heretical kind to give vent to imagination in an attempt to strengthen their unorthodox position. The evidence from this source therefore lacks historical validity, but it does, by way of contrast, bring out vividly the remarkably restrained nature of the canonical testimony to Christ.

Some fragmentary evidence has been preserved of a gospel (the *Hebrew Gospel*) which cannot be classed as heretical and which may preserve some genuine material not found in the canonical gospels. An examination of the most likely passages (see Dunkerly, *op. cit.*, 102 ff.) shows some interesting deviations. For instance, Jesus' mother and brethren urge Him to be baptized with them by John the Baptist, but Jesus hesitates because of His sinlessness. Some dogmatic consideration seems to have entered. Most of the other sayings possess a secondary looking character which suggests the need for caution in accepting them as genuine.

4. *Gnostic Works*

Little need be said about Gnostic sources as a possible quarry for authentic sayings of Jesus. The most notable books which preserve sayings of a similar kind to those in the gospels are the *Gospel of Thomas* and the *Gospel of Philip*. The parallels in the former alone warrant serious attention. There are many which echo the thought of the synoptic gospels, and in these cases it is almost certain that the author has used the canonical gospels, although there have been various other theories to account for the parallels (cf. the discussion of R. M. Wilson, *Studies in the Gospel of Thomas* [1960]). The possibility of some independently authentic material being preserved in Gnostic circles cannot be entirely ruled out. Probability is strongly against it, for in this work some of the known sayings of Jesus have been adapted for gnostic purposes and this tendency may well have led to the creation of other sayings. Gnostics are not a safe source for authentic teaching. The early Fathers constantly charged them with distorting the Scriptures. Would any genuine oral tradition have escaped?

5

The Early Life and Ministry of Jesus Christ

It is impossible to produce a biography of Jesus as understood by the modern use of that term. Since Christianity is a historic religion, it is essential to provide at least an outline of the main events which went to make up His earthly life. It will be valuable by way of introduction to give a summary of the main stages of the story as it can be reconstructed from the gospels.

1. *The Thirty Years in Nazareth.* Although this lasted for so many years, the material preserved is confined to the birth stories and one brief incident when Jesus was twelve.

2. *The Period of Preparation.* This covers the ministry of John the Baptist in heralding the coming of Christ.

3. *The Judaean Ministry.* This includes the earliest period of the Lord's work until the commencement of the Galilean ministry.

4. *The Galilean Ministry.* This section may be divided for convenience into three periods. The first ends with the choosing of the Twelve, the second with the withdrawal of Jesus from northern Galilee, and the third with His departure for Jerusalem on His last journey.

5. *The Closing Period of the Ministry.* This is a convenient heading for the material fitted into the journey to the time when Jesus enters Jerusalem, mainly centered beyond Jordan.

6. *The Passion and Resurrection Narratives.* Under this caption are included all the events from the entry into Jerusalem until the resurrection and the various post-resurrection appearances of Jesus to His disciples, culminating with the Ascension.

In the following outline of events and teaching, it is intended to fill out in considerable detail these main stages to bring into focus the major purpose of Jesus. It is important to recognize that the theology of Jesus is seen both in His acts and in His teaching. An over-concentration on one or the other would have been a mistake. They are inextricably linked. The many deeds of compassion, the demonstrations of power, the human interest, are all part of the total picture, and form the background of the teaching. At the same time the teaching throws light upon the true nature and interpretation of the acts. Nevertheless, in the outline itself the emphasis will be on the events, since a separate section will deal with the teaching, both in method and content.

1. *The Thirty Years in Nazareth*

The most important part of this preliminary section of the life of Jesus is His advent into human life. It is for this reason that Matthew and Luke begin with narratives relating to the birth of Jesus, while John goes back and reflects upon His eternal pre-existence. One would not expect the story of Jesus to begin where John begins, for he sets the scene beyond the realm of history. Nevertheless, by reason of what the evangelists believed Jesus to be, his is the most logical beginning.

a. *John's Prologue* (John 1:1-18). At first glance it seems strange that John should introduce his book with statements about the Word, especially as he does not identify the Word as Jesus Christ until toward the end of the Prologue. Evidently the first readers of the gospel would have known what John was describing, otherwise his opening would have been more mystifying than elucidating. One cannot now be certain of its source for John. Philo of Alexandria has much to say about the Logos, which in his system was an intermediary principle between God and man, but he denied the possibility of the Logos becoming flesh. When John says that the Logos did become flesh he is clearly presenting a different kind of Logos from Philo. For all his great erudition, Philo could not present a Logos capable of dwelling among men, who could move men into action and give power to men to become sons of God. This was a new element in the contemporary Greek world. Jewish thought had also prepared for the coming of Jesus, not only with the Messianic hope, but by its concept of the intermediary Memra, God's agent in the world of creation.

Far more important than the origin of the idea of the Word are the statements concerning Him which John makes in his

Prologue. Not only does he stress His pre-existence, but also His divine nature. His power is evidence of His creative energy and of His re-creative activity. The Word is identified as Light shining in an atmosphere of darkness, which describes the moral environment into which Jesus came. The Word becoming flesh is pivotal to John's introduction to his gospel. The whole account is basically a human and historic story, because the becoming flesh had taken place among men and the glory of the incarnate Word had been seen. There is an unquestionable connection between the Prologue and the events that follow. The same Jesus Christ, whose actions and words are recorded is the means whereby grace and truth come to men, and through whom God makes known His revelation. Unless the records of all the gospels are seen in the light of this mission, there can be no proper evaluation of the life of Jesus.

One significant feature about John's introduction is the mention of John by name, the witness to the Light, before the Light had Himself been identified. This shows, in agreement with the synoptic gospels, the importance of the ministry of John the Baptist.

b. *The Birth Narratives* (Matt. 1 and 2; Luke 1:1-2:38). John's statement that the Word became flesh at once raises the question in what circumstances it happened. Matthew and Luke supply the answer. The narratives, although brief, are nevertheless sufficient to establish the historical reality of the incarnation. There is a restraint about them that immediately impresses. Matthew approaches the subject from a different point of view than Luke, and yet their narratives are complementary to each other. Both stress the supernatural character of the advent of Jesus. In Matthew this is brought out by the narration of several dreams which reveal various stages of development, from the announcement of Joseph's reaction when he learns of Mary's pregnancy until the return from Egypt. In Luke's account a similar impression is created by the angel's announcement to Mary. It is at once clear that this is no ordinary birth. It is not surprising therefore that Matthew records a citation that a virgin would conceive (Matt. 1:23). It is true that Isaiah's statement need not refer to a virgin, but to a young woman, but it is equally evident that Matthew intended the readers to understand that the advent of Jesus was effected in a miraculous way by conception taking place in a virgin. Luke's account supports this in the promise to Mary that the Holy Spirit should come upon her (Luke 1:35).

It is never suggested in these narratives or anywhere else in the gospels that people generally regarded Jesus as any other than the son of Joseph (cf. John 6:4; Matt. 13:55; Luke 2:27, 41, 43). Popular opinion is no sure guide to truth, and both Matthew and Luke have set out to stress the uniqueness of the birth of Jesus as a necessary prelude to their accounts of His life and ministry. Whatever modern attempts may be made to approach the life of Jesus from a purely human point of view, it is beyond dispute that the evangelists made no such attempt.

In Matthew's gospel the Annunciation is made to Joseph and the most characteristic feature of the revelation made to him is the clear statement of the purpose of the advent. Jesus was coming to save His people from their sins (Matt. 1:21). At the beginning of the gospel a theological note is introduced. The subsequent doings of Jesus are all geared to this purpose, which provides their motive force.

In Luke's gospel the Annunciation is to Mary and is accompanied by an account of the promise of the birth of John the Baptist and its fulfillment. The most significant feature of this account is the inclusion of the hymns known as the Magnificat and Benedictus, both of which are formed on the pattern of the Old Testament Psalms. They create an atmosphere of rejoicing over the coming of Jesus that is frequently reflected in the subsequent narrative, for Luke's account has more references to joy than any of the others.

The story of the angel's announcement to the shepherds draws attention to the same feature. The day of the advent of Jesus was a day of good tidings of great joy. At the same time, the announcement was made of peace on earth to all men of good will, which gives a distinctly universal aspect to the purpose of Jesus. The mission of Jesus could never be understood against a background of narrow nationalistic aspirations. It needed a broader canvas. The homage of humble shepherds signifies something of the receptivity of the common people, a feature which was to be abundantly illustrated in the subsequent ministry of Jesus.

Matthew's account of the homage of the wise men presents a rather different aspect. These were Gentile inquirers for the coming Christ. They believed themselves to have been divinely led, and indeed through being supernaturally warned of Herod's devices were able to frustrate his intention to take adverse action against the child Jesus. This homage of Gentiles is specially noteworthy at the beginning of a gospel which is primarily written with Jewish interests in mind. The Messiah was not so Jewish that Gentiles had no desire to worship Him, and in harmony with this is the conclusion of this same gospel, in which the commission of Jesus to His disciples is world-wide.

It is not possible to be certain when the wise men arrived at the place where Jesus was. Some think it was a considerable time after His birth, a view based mainly on the evidence that Herod sought to kill all the children under two years old. Herod did not know how long ago the child had been born. He knew only when the star appeared. The flight into Egypt, recorded only in Matthew 2:13, 14, is seen as a direct fulfillment of prophecy. This therefore plays an important part in Matthew's purpose, i.e., to show that the course of the life of Jesus was no accidental happening, but a designed fulfillment of what God had foretold.

In the meantime, Jesus was present at the Temple for circumcision when eight days old, according to Jewish custom (Luke 2:22 ff.). On this occasion Simeon and Anna both bore witness to Jesus. Simeon's song (Nunc Dimittis) again conveys a universal viewpoint, for Jesus was to become a Light for Gentile illumination (2:32) as well as Israel's glory. At the same time, Simeon foresaw hostility toward Jesus, for some would speak evil against Him (2:34). Both Simeon and Anna typify the realization of the fulfillment in Jesus of long awaited Messianic hopes. The story of the ministry of Jesus is intended to be read against such a background.

Both Matthew and Luke include genealogies. Matthew uses one to introduce his gospel, tracing the list from Abraham to Jesus. Luke, who does not refer to the genealogy until after recording the ministry of John the Baptist (Luke 3), begins with Jesus and traces His ancestry back to Adam. Although some of the names in these two genealogical lists are the same, most of them are not. A partial explanation may be found in the schematic arrangement adopted by Matthew, having three groups of fourteen names (Matt. 1:17). This is made possible only by various omissions. It has been suggested that whereas Matthew follows the lineage of Joseph, Luke follows Mary's, but this supposition seems to run counter to what Luke himself states, since he does not even mention Mary. It is impossible to tell either the sources of these genealogies or the extent to which either author depended upon his own investigations. The major contribution of both lists for the life of Jesus is clear enough – both trace the ancestry through David and Abraham. He came of a royal line which gave rise to the title Son of David, which was used by various people in the course of the narrative.

Of all the evangelists it is only Luke who makes any attempt to set the record of Jesus on the stage of secular history. Even he concentrates on the timing of the appearance of John the Baptist rather than on the appearance of Jesus, although he shows the two events to be inseparable. The dating is sixfold (Luke 3:1, 2) and points to the major political figures in the Jewish world. This note of Luke's is of great importance in establishing the historical setting of Christianity.

One other contact with secular history which is mentioned by Luke, is the census of Quirinius, governor of Syria (2:2), which is said to be the occasion for Mary and Joseph to travel to Bethlehem just prior to the birth of Jesus. There is known to have been a census held under this official in A.D. 6, but this would be too late for the birth of Jesus. There is some reason to think that an earlier census was held in Syria more approximate to Luke's chronology, but the difficulty of Quirinius still remains, unless, as Sir William Ramsay supposed, this official held an extraordinary command at the same time as the governorship of Varus.

c. *Home Life at Nazareth* (Luke 2:39-52). Contrary to the modern idea of biographical studies that seeks traces from the early years of influences which contributed to the later development of a character, none of the evangelists shows the slightest interest in early environmental factors. Luke alone mentions an incident during the thirty years that Jesus spent in Nazareth. The visit to the Temple when Jesus was twelve was no doubt included to draw attention to the fact that in the home of Jesus the usual Jewish practices were observed. Twelve was the age at which Jewish boys attended the Passover feast. For Luke it had more significance than this because of the opportunity it afforded to illustrate Jesus' first contact with the Temple teachers.

The incident not only reveals their amazement at the wisdom of Jesus, but also His own consciousness of a divine mission, which His family did not understand. They evidently were incapable of appreciating His fullness of wisdom and His possession of special divine grace (2:40). Mary appears to have understood most, but she kept her reflections to herself (2:51). She must have wondered often at the grace with which He was subject to her. The restraint of the canonical account of the childhood of Jesus contrasts vividly with the spate of childish stories which were later current in the apocryphal gospels. The processes of thought by which Jesus arrived at His Messianic consciousness may claim the interest of some modern theologians, but were never considered important by the evangelists.

In the body of the gospels there are a few hints given of the attitude of the inhabitants of Nazareth toward Jesus. He was known as the carpenter or the carpenter's son (Mark 6:3; Matt. 13:55). Moreover, there were other children in the family – James, Joses, Simon, Judas and some sisters (Matt. 13:55, 56). None of the Nazareth inhabitants apparently expected Jesus to show much wisdom or to do mighty works, for they were astonished when His ministry was in progress. The mystery of the hidden years is deepened by the obvious hardness of the people who knew Him best.

2. *The Period of Preparation*

Before the actual commencement of the ministry of Jesus, there were several significant events – the preaching of John the Baptist, the baptism and temptation of Jesus. All three of these events are of basic importance for the records of the public ministry of Jesus in the synoptic gospels, although Mark makes only a passing reference to the Temptation.

a. *John the Baptist* (Matt. 3:1-12; Mark 1:1-8; Luke 3:1-17). The ministry of John the Baptist must be considered in the light of contemporary Judaism. There was certainly the expectation of the dawning of a new age, and Messianic hopes. There was belief in the approach of the Kingdom of God, although popular ideas were mostly materialistic, but John did not follow the normal pattern. In his methods and teaching he was like one of the ancient prophets. In many respects he was the last of an era. He was this only because he was able to point to the Inaugurator of another era and the dawn of a new Kingdom. All three synoptic writers mention the testimony of Isaiah to the coming of John the Baptist. The link with the past is thus established and a divine authority is given to the work of the herald of Jesus. All the writers record the preparatory ministry of the Baptist, but it is Luke in particular who carries on the quotation from Isaiah to include the promise that all flesh should see God's salvation. The records clearly bring out John the Baptist's call to repent, and his prediction of the Coming One who would be greater than he, and would baptize with the Holy Spirit. Both Matthew and Luke further call attention to the judgment which would follow the arrival of the One to come.

When John preached a baptism of repentance, there was immediate criticism of the Pharisees and Sadducees, who were described as a generation of vipers, a particularly strong expression of adverse opinion which was intended to bring them to a state of true repentance. There is a forthrightness and sternness about John's message which showed the serious character of his preparatory work. With such a herald as he, whose clothing of camel's hair drew attention to the sternness of his character, the coming of Jesus was set against a morally challenging situation. Men were being prepared by the serious call to repentance. Moreover, the challenge to moral reformation was made specific by the Baptist, as Luke brings out clearly by samples of the advice given to tax collectors and soldiers.

The rite of baptism was not new with John. The Jews practiced proselyte baptism, and some groups, e.g., the Essenes, appear to have practiced ritual cleansing, which was closely akin to initiatory baptism. The group at Qumran placed some importance on the rite, and it is interesting to conjecture whether John had had personal contact with the community. If he had previously done this, he had certainly departed from their pattern, for they were essentially inward-looking and their rites were exclusively for initiates; John was essentially outward-looking, directing his call for repentance to the multitudes. According to Matthew's account, he announced the imminence of the Kingdom of heaven in the same terms that Jesus began to preach. This is clearly intended to show the continuity between the preaching of both, although the fundamental difference between them is that Jesus is Himself the Inaugurator of the Kingdom, whereas John was only the herald.

b. *The Baptism of Jesus* (Matt. 3:13-17; Mark 1:9-11; Luke 3:21, 22). The baptism of Jesus is the climax of John's work. When the king arrived, the herald's work was done. John was expecting to announce Jesus, but he never expected that Jesus would present Himself for baptism. The one he was expecting was surely beyond the need for repentance. His greatness was such that John felt himself unworthy to unloose His sandals. Why did He request a baptism of repentance? Matthew alone records John's hesitation and for this reason some scholars have regarded this as a later addition, prompted by motives of reverence, but in view of John's overwhelming conviction that Jesus was infinitely greater than he, it would have been much more surprising if no hesitation had been recorded. At the same time the reason for Jesus' action must be considered. According to Matthew, it was to fulfill all righteousness (Matt. 3:15), by which Jesus made clear to John that it was the right and proper thing for Him to be baptized.

The problem arises concerning Jesus' submission to a rite which was specifically described as a baptism of repentance for the remission of sins. None of the synoptic evangelists gives the explanation, but all record the attestation of the heavenly voice bearing witness to the beloved Son in whom the Father is well pleased. The identification of Jesus with those needing repentance was clearly part of the divine plan. For the multitudes the baptismal rite symbolized their desire to forsake their sins, but for Jesus it meant a call to identify Himself with a sinful people. Neither John nor any of the witnesses could recognize the theological implications of this symbolic act. It was part of the process that Paul later recognized, in which Christ was made sin for mankind (II Cor. 5:21).

Undoubtedly all the evangelists see the baptism as the commencement of the public ministry of Jesus. This is marked especially by the descent of the Spirit upon Him (in the form of a dove) and by the heavenly attestation. This differentiated Jesus from all others who attended John's baptism. It is improbable that these supernatural signs were seen by any apart from John and Jesus, but for the evangelists their importance lay in their revelation of the nature of the mission of Jesus. John's gospel is most specific of all in recording the remarkable pronouncement of John the Baptist that Jesus was the Lamb of God who takes away the world's sin (John 1:29). The writer of the gospel gives no indication of the extent of the Baptist's own understanding of his statement, although he clearly sees its importance in distinguishing the Baptist's work from that of Jesus. The fact that later doubts gripped the mind of the Baptist regarding the claims of Jesus does not vitiate his confident prediction at the commencement of the ministry.

c. *The Temptation of Jesus* (Matt. 4:1-11; Mark 1:12, 13; Luke 4:1-13). This was perhaps the most revealing event in the preparatory period. The fact that it followed immediately from the baptism is regarded as significant by all the synoptic evangelists. As Jesus had identified Himself with sinners in John's baptism, so He exposed Himself to the temptings of the devil. It would be better to speak of testings rather than temptations, since the latter word has too often become associated with a yielding approach which was certainly not present in the case of Jesus. Details of the characteristics of the testings which came to Him are given only by Matthew and Luke, although Mark mentions some important features, such as the presence of wild beasts and the ministration of angels.

In all the accounts the idea of a supernatural conflict is inescapable and clearly forms a basic introduction to the later Passion narratives, in which the climax of the conflict is enacted: The three temptations mentioned by Matthew and Luke are to be regarded not as exhaustive but as exemplary. They are typical of the avenues along which testings continually come. They are, moreover, not to be restricted to the period of forty days, as Luke makes clear when he mentions that the devil's withdrawal was until a convenient season. The course of the ministry frequently presented occasions in which the testings would be repeated.

To understand the temptations, account must be taken of the Messianic consciousness of Jesus. He was deeply aware of His mission and His power to accomplish it. The testings concerned the methods He would use to accomplish it. The use of miraculous power for His own preservation (to turn stone to bread) was rejected as totally unworthy of His mission. It would amount to a failure to maintain true priorities. Moreover, the urge to use the same miraculous powers to impress upon the world at large His Messianic claims was equally alien to His true purpose. It would appeal to the spectacular, but would be diametrically opposed to the divine methods.

The other recorded testing concerned the character of the Kingdom which Jesus had come to inaugurate. Was it to be comparable to the kingdoms of this world? Was it to share its glory with theirs? Such a possibility was unthinkable, and would amount to conceding allegiance to the devil, in whose hands, as Jesus acknowledged, were the imperial ambitions of the present age. His Kingdom was of a totally different order.

In all three of the temptations recorded, the Lord overcomes the tempting of the devil by means of the Scriptures, as the most appropriate medium for establishing the principles of divine action.

The difference in order of the temptations in Matthew and Luke are more significant for the respective purpose of each than for the consciousness of Jesus Himself. Matthew places the temptation to an earthly imperial status last, probably because of his design to show the true kingly status of Jesus, while Luke places last the urge to self-display because of his desire to show Jesus as essentially a man among men. Whether either knew the precise order or whether either attached any special importance to it is impossible to say.

The record of these temptations is generally appealed to as evidence that Jesus was in all respects tempted as men are (cf. Heb. 4:15), but this is true in only a limited respect. Since Jesus alone possessed Messianic consciousness and power, the testings which came to Him were unique. But it cannot be denied that they are allied to those which afflict all men. It must be recognized that Jesus was exposed to many more temptations than those recorded, which must be regarded as typical.

The public ministry of Jesus opened against a background of tremendous struggle and a resolute rejection of all methods of achieving His mission which were opposed to the real purpose for which He came.

3. *The Judaean Ministry of Jesus*

It is in John's gospel alone that any information is given about the early Judaean ministry, a fact which raises some problems but which need not lead to historical skepticism regarding this period. It may, in fact, be stated that the accounts in the other gospels would be unintelligible apart from John's account of the initial introduction of the disciples to Jesus. This followed immediately upon the impact of the preaching of John the Baptist upon them (John 1:19 ff.). They may not have understood the full importance of the pronouncement about the Lamb of God, if they had any insight at all, which is certainly questionable. They were drawn as by a magnet to the Person about whom the words were spoken.

It is significant that John does not record a mass following, but rather the response of individuals. Discipleship was at this stage loose and needed confirmation by a further specific call later on, as the synoptic gospels record. There is no doubt about the deep impression made by Jesus. He was acclaimed as Messiah by His first two followers. He was acknowledged as Son of God and King of Israel by Nathanael. He was winning men by means utterly different from those suggested by Satan at the time of the Temptation.

During this period of personal contact with future apostles Jesus made a visit to Galilee, and while there He was involved in a wedding at Cana, which is noted by the evangelist as being the place of the first of Jesus' signs (John 2:1-11). The purpose of the signs was to reveal the glory of Christ, and it is not without meaning that the first sample should be in a purely domestic setting. It throws light upon the humanity of Jesus.

Two other incidents in Jerusalem preceded the opening of the public ministry in Galilee. The first was a public act, the second a private conversation. The cleansing of the Temple by the expulsion of money changers (John 2:13 ff.) was a daring commencement to public work, and for this reason many prefer to regard this incident as misplaced by John, especially in view of the similar incident recorded by the synoptics at the end of the ministry. A double cleansing cannot be dismissed as impossible, although many regard it as improbable. Some consider it to be symbolic of the purifying purpose of Jesus in the citadel of contemporary Judaism. John clearly regarded the historical details as important, for he mentions the Passover feast. The incident itself reveals the great authority which the presence of Jesus must have conveyed. It also illuminates one aspect of the mission of Jesus for He alludes to His coming resurrection (as John 2:18 ff. shows).

The conversation with Nicodemus (John 3) is of a different order, although akin insofar as Nicodemus was himself associated with official Judaism. His quest was typical of those who were dissatisfied with their religion, and yet who were mystified by the spiritual emphasis of Jesus. The dialogue which John relates is important as showing the place of regeneration in the thought of Jesus and the inability of Nicodemus to grasp its true meaning. This was to be symbolic of the reaction of men generally to the spiritual message of Jesus.

John's account brings out clearly the connection between the work of Jesus and John the Baptist. Both practiced baptism in the Jordan. This similarity caused difficulties among John's disciples (John 3:25), who were unable to grasp the preparatory character of John's work, and necessitated a repetition of John's denial that he was the Messiah. He was only a witness, and his testimony agreed with the self-testimony of Jesus Himself.

When Jesus left Judaea for Galilee to commence His ministry there, He passed through Samaria, and His experiences, recorded only by John, are a significant introduction to the synoptic account of the ministry (John 4:1-45). Samaria had little in common with Jerusalem except for possessing its own central worship and maintaining some kind of Messianic hope. The Jews and Samaritans had no personal dealings with each other, as John makes clear. All the more remarkable, therefore, was the Lord's interview with a Samaritan woman. It proves beyond doubt that He had no intention of being restricted by narrow Jewish nationalism. It shows furthermore that His approach to women differed from that of His Jewish contemporaries. His conversation with this woman revealed His extraordinary insight into human nature, and it has since become a pattern for personal evangelism.

The most striking feature about the whole incident is the self-revelation of Jesus. He acknowledged Himself to be the Messiah (John 4:26), in spite of the fact that He later showed a consistent refusal to permit His disciples to make this known. It appears that He took a different line with the Samaritans because their Messianic hope differed from that of the Jews. It was not so closely tied to nationalistic aspirations and was therefore less open to serious misapprehensions. Moreover, the sequel to the conversation shows the spiritual character of the Lord's mission in the manifest joy that He had when people believed on Him. The dialogue itself supports this view, since Jesus soon turns the conversation away from material to spiritual concerns, especially the spiritual nature of God.

6

The Galilean Ministry

After the events in Samaria Jesus returns to the place where water was turned into wine and performs another miracle there. Although a similar incident is recorded in the synoptic gospels later on in the ministry, it is best to regard the miracle related by John (4:46-53) as distinct, for several differences in detail suggest this. Moreover, John points out specifically that this was the second of Jesus' signs in Galilee, as if he were attaching some importance to this fact.

The healing of the official's son at Capernaum serves as a fitting prelude to the whole Galilean ministry, for Jesus has not yet become well-known in Galilee for His miraculous works, and this fact heightens all the more the father's faith, which is specifically mentioned as a factor in the healing.

It has already been noted that the Galilean ministry may be divided into three periods, and these will be separately described. It should be observed, however, that although the general heading relates to Galilee, there must have been some activity in Jerusalem, if John's record is to be taken into account. Most of the time, however, Jesus worked and taught in Galilee.

1. *The Period up to the Choosing of the Twelve*

a. *The Initial Call of Disciples.* The choosing of the Twelve began in the specific calling of four men from their fishing, Peter and Andrew, James and John (Matt. 4:18-22; Mark 1:16-20; Luke 5:1-11). From John's account one can see that these men had earlier contact with Jesus, but now they are called to devote themselves more wholeheartedly to His work. In the process of time others were added, but it was not until the number had reached twelve that Jesus appointed them as an officially constituted body of apostles, which did not occur until the end of this period. Connected with the call of the first disciples is the incident of the miraculous catch of fish (Luke 5:1-11), which is intended to emphasize the superior achievement of catching men. The spiritual is more excellent than the material.

It is impossible to be certain about the exact order of events in this period, and it is consequently better to group the main incidents into similar categories. With this in mind, the call of Levi will be mentioned, although not occurring until later on in the period (Matt. 9:9-13; Mark 2:13-17; Luke 5:27-32). Levi, who became known as Matthew, is representative of a class of people greatly despised in the contemporary Jewish world. He was a tax collector, and since taxes were a sore point with the Jews, those who collected them became the targets for social contempt. No information is given about the grounds on which Jesus based His choice of men, but many of them seem to have been unlikely characters. It is one of the most illuminating studies to consider how He molded such men for His purpose.

b. *The Sermon on the Mount* (Matt. 5-7). Another important aspect of the early ministry of Jesus was His preaching, and it is mainly Matthew who gives samples, particularly in his long discourse known as the Sermon on the Mount. In view of the fact that Luke records much of this discourse material in isolated passages, many scholars dispute whether Matthew's material was delivered on one occasion. It is possible that Matthew is responsible for the collection of the material into a discourse, but this is by no means certain. He undoubtedly leads his readers to assume that one particular occasion was in mind. Moreover, it is reasonable to maintain that the Lord frequently repeated the same teaching, as was customary among Jewish rabbis, and in this case there is no basis for disputing the unity of the Sermon on the Mount. The content is more important, however, than this historical question. Since a separate section is devoted to a general summary of the teaching of Jesus, it will be necessary only to indicate the special characteristics of this important discourse.

The main emphasis is ethical. Jesus had in mind the establishment of His Kingdom and the consequent need of new patterns of behavior. His own teaching is set forth as an advance on the teaching of Moses. A wide variety of themes is covered, mostly of a social character, such as murder, divorce, retaliation, and attitudes toward one's enemies. There are, however, many sayings which deal with personal religious motives, such as prayer and fasting, self-deception, and varying reactions to the hearing of the Word. The Beatitudes at the beginning of the discourse similarly encourage spiritual and moral values. Matthew records what the hearers thought of the sermon. They were astonished, and this may be regarded as typical during the early ministry. It was the authoritative nature of the teaching which so deeply impressed the hearers.

c. *Healings and Other Miracles.* There were during this period many acts of healing, of which various samples are recorded. Matthew, particularly, groups the healing miracles (Matt. 8:1-9:8; cf. Mark 1:40-2:12; Luke 5:12-26). He places the following incidents in a sequence. The healing of the leper (Matt. 8:1-4), the centurion's servant (8:5-13), Peter's mother-in-law (8:14, 15), the sick in the evening (8:16, 17), the Gadarene demoniac (8:28-34), the palsied man (9:1-8), Jairus' daughter and the woman with a hemorrhage (9:18-26), two blind men (9:27-31), and the dumb demoniac (9:32-34). Most of these healings appear also in Mark and Luke, but in a different order. Matthew's arrangement vividly emphasizes the nature of the healing ministry. Although not mentioned in every case, there is frequent reference to the faith of the people healed. In the case of the paralytic the power of Jesus to forgive sins is linked with His power to heal (Matt. 9:2). This is a reminder that the spiritual ministry was of more concern to Jesus than the healing work. None of the gospels presents Him as a wonder-worker. The miracles of healing are related to bring out the element of compassion. The attention is focused on the human aspects and not on the extraordinary nature of the cure. There is no suggestion of magic, nor are there any incantations or formulas. Jesus is always master of the situation (see later section on the miracles of Jesus).

Of special importance is the power of Jesus over evil spirits, for this is a marked feature of all stages of the ministry. The work of Jesus was set in an atmosphere of spiritual conflict. The examples quoted showing His power over demoniacs are to be regarded as illustrations of spiritual victories.

During this earlier period of the ministry, one miracle is

recorded which affected the world of nature, i.e., the stilling of the storm (Matt. 8:23-27; cf. Mark 4:35-41; Luke 8:22-25). It is placed earlier in Matthew than in the other synoptics. The focus of attention is once again not so much on the marvelous power of Jesus as on the lack of faith on the part of the disciples. Nonetheless, the element of marvel is not absent, as the miracle caused the disciples to discuss what kind of man He was that the wind and sea obeyed Him (Matt. 8:27; Mark 4:41; Luke 8:25). Throughout the gospel story there is an element of mystery about the person of Jesus.

d. *Popularity and Criticism.* The evangelists are deeply interested in the impact Jesus made on various types of people. This is most marked in their comments on the early popularity of Jesus. Matthew's summary in 4:23-25 makes this clear – His fame spread throughout all Syria (cf. Mark 1:28). This enthusiasm over His healing work was undoubtedly superficial. The real meaning of His message, and the self-effacing spiritual character of His mission had not yet dawned upon the multitudes, nor were they capable of comprehending it. By way of contrast with this superficial popularity, the criticism of the Pharisees is brought out in equally clear fashion. Mark, in fact, preserves a sequence of incidents which is designed to show the increasing hostility of the scribes and Pharisees (Mark 2:1-3:6). The culmination of this sequence shows the intensity of the hostility since the Pharisees joined forces with the Herodians, a combination which rarely happened.

At a later stage of the ministry, Jesus makes some pointed criticisms of the Pharisees, mainly on the grounds of their hypocrisy (cf. Matt. 23). At this early stage, however, He presents them with a reasoned approach to provide them with the opportunity to respond. The stumbling-stone for them was the unorthodoxy of Jesus. In their eyes He was a law-breaker in His attitude toward the Sabbath, while His social fellowship with tax collectors and sinners could only invite Pharisaic contempt. No doubt the Pharisees soon reacted to the popular opinion that Jesus taught and acted with authority, in contrast to the scribes (Matt. 7:29). They could not fail to see a very dangerous threat to their own grip upon the common people.

e. *The Choosing of the Twelve.* The naming of twelve specially chosen disciples and the description of their first mission is of such importance that all the synoptic gospels mention them. In both Matthew and Mark (Matt. 10:1; Mark 3:13-19) the commissioning is linked with authority over unclean spirits. In addition to this, Matthew mentions the power to heal, and Mark the command to preach. Luke separates the story of the choosing of the Twelve from the special purpose of the office of apostle (cf. Luke 6:12-16; 9:1, 2). The men whom Jesus chose were a representative group. They were not all drawn from the poorer classes, for the father of James and John possessed his own boat and employed servants (Mark 1:20). Matthew as a tax-collector would be well-to-do, although hated by his compatriots. Simon may have been an erstwhile revolutionary.

Such importance did Jesus attach to the mission of the Twelve that He gave them specific instructions which served not only for their immediate benefit on their first preaching tour, but also as a pattern for the subsequent missions of the Christian church. The charge to the Twelve is more fully recorded in Matthew than in the other gospels (Matt. 10:5 ff.; cf. Luke 9:1-6; and Mark 6:7-13). Special emphasis is placed on material provisions, for Jesus advises that nothing unnecessary should be taken. The disciples are instructed how to proceed if any town or village receives them, and what to do if it does not. The advice is essentially practical. The message they are to proclaim is confined to an announcement of the nearness of the Kingdom. They were not to imagine that all would warm to this message, for much hostility and persecution would await them.

The advice is obviously to prepare Jesus' disciples for future rather than immediate opposition and is well illustrated from the story of the early church. To fortify them they are reminded of the certainty of their heavenly Father's care over them. The most startling prediction given to the Twelve was the certainty that the message of Jesus would result in serious division within households. He who had Himself experienced the hostility of the Pharisees, even during this initial period, was in no doubt concerning the difficulties which would confront His disciples. Victory would not come except through enduring much for Christ's sake.

Some comment has already been made on the relationship between Jesus and John the Baptist, but Matthew and Luke include further sayings of Jesus on the subject which deserves notice. It has been seen that Jesus began by preaching what John had preached, but He soon went on to proclaim His unique message. John had already recognized and publicly announced Jesus to be greater than he, but it is not surprising that he became perplexed by later developments. When doubts arose, he sent messengers from his prison, where he had been incarcerated by Herod, to ascertain whether Jesus was prepared to confirm His Messiahship (Matt. 11:2 ff.). Not only did Jesus send an encouraging word back to John, but also commended him for his greatness in the hearing of the crowds. The difference between John and Jesus is illustrated by Jesus Himself from the children's games of funerals and weddings. He points out that His own generation was satisfied with neither.

2. *The Period up to the Withdrawal of Jesus From Northern Galilee*

a. *Sabbath Controversies and Healings.* It is convenient at this point to include the incident recorded only by John, when an impotent man was healed at the pool of Bethesda. It is impossible to identify the feast during which the healing occurred (John 5:1) and equally impossible to know precisely where to place this incident within the synoptic framework. Its main significance is in the fact that the man's own attitude of faith is not specifically stated, although it is clearly implied by his ready response to the command from Jesus to take up his bed and walk. Since the miracle was performed on the Sabbath, the action again aroused the antagonism of the Jews, although in this case was added the further charge that Jesus made Himself equal with God.

Another Sabbath controversy occurred when the disciples plucked ears of grain from a grainfield on the Sabbath (Matt. 12:1-8; Mark 2:23-28; Luke 6:1-5), an action which Pharisaic casuistry regarded as work and was therefore forbidden. This led to a specific claim by Jesus to be "lord of the sabbath" (Matt. 12:8), which placed Him in a superior position to the scribes in the interpretation of the Law. Again the plot of the Pharisees to destroy Jesus is mentioned (12:14), after another healing on the Sabbath day.

During the course of his accounts of healing miracles Matthew refers to the fulfillment of prophecy, citing a passage from the Servant songs of Isaiah (Matt. 12:15-21). This is an important aspect of his record of Jesus' ministry, but it is also seen to a lesser extent in all the gospels. Luke records two outstanding miracles which occurred during this period, the healing of the centurion's servant at Capernaum (Luke 7:1-10) and the raising of the widow's son at Nain (7:11-17). The first is remarkable for the faith of a non-Israelite who was prepared to believe the authoritative word of Jesus, and the second for the effect it had upon the crowds, who glorified God (7:16).

An incident which shows the deep human understanding of Jesus is the anointing of His feet by a woman, well-known for her sinful character, in the house of a Pharisee (7:36-50). Luke vividly tells the story of the woman's devotion and of the Pharisee's carping criticisms. By means of a parable Jesus shows Simon the Pharisee that the woman, in spite of her known character, had nevertheless outshone him in devotion. Such an incident is an acted parable of the effect of Jesus on the two representative groups, the religious and the non-religious. Those who should have set an example in devotion dismally failed, while the underprivileged responded.

b. *Division and Attack.* Controversies were never far away in the ministry of Jesus, but one of the most pointed of these followed the exorcism of a devil (Matt. 12:22 ff.; Mark 3:20 ff.; Luke 11:14-23). The Pharisees attributed it to Beelzebub, prince of the devils, but Jesus points out how ludicrous it is to think of Satan casting out Satan. The power to cast out demons is by the Spirit of God. Never more vividly than this did the spiritual character of the conflict come to the fore. The tragedy was that the Pharisees with all their religious scrupulosity were near to committing the unpardonable sin. Some of the scribes and Pharisees then pursued a different line against Jesus – the demand for a sign, which He emphatically rejected. He was so essentially different from the Messianic concept of the Jews that it is not surprising that they required a sign to resolve their perplexity. But they were too blind to take notice of earlier signs, e.g., Jonah and Solomon.

It was necessary now for Jesus to make clear His true relationship to His family, and He shows the development of a relationship which far transcends family ties (Matt. 12:46-50).

c. *Samples of the Teaching of Jesus.* The teaching of Jesus remained much the same as in the earlier period. Luke records many sayings parallel to those in the Sermon on the Mount, although in a different context. There is no doubt that Jesus frequently repeated the same sayings, and there is no need therefore to identify Luke's sermon with Matthew's. The common people who gladly listened to Jesus needed constant repetition of the teaching. Luke records some material common with Matthew, but his sermon is brief, and even in the common material shows a fair amount of variation in the wording. Acknowledgment of the fact that much of the teaching material was given on a number of occasions supports the contention that in some respects the teaching methods of the rabbis influenced the method of Jesus (cf. B. Gerhardsson's *Memory and Manuscript* [1961]). The uniqueness of Jesus' teaching material and method must, nevertheless, be fully acknowledged. He understood better than the rabbis the psychology of teaching.

Luke gives an interesting insight into one aspect of Jesus' life at this period. Not only was He accompanied by the Twelve, but also by a group of women, some of whom were wealthy enough to supply means of support for the company (Luke 8:1-3).

Several parables of the Kingdom were taught by Jesus in the course of His preaching tours. It is Matthew who shows a special interest in these and collects them into a group (Matt. 13). Since a discussion of the parabolic teaching of Jesus will be included elsewhere, it will be sufficient to point out the significance of this method of teaching in this particular period of the ministry. Crowds were still flocking to hear Jesus, but the basic receptivity was varied. The parable of the Sower (or more accurately the parable of the Soils) was intended to show Jesus' recognition of this fact in His own ministry, and also illustrates what the disciples might expect. The choice of the parabolic method was itself intended to show that Jesus had a selective purpose in His teaching. Vivid stories would be most readily stored in the mind, but their significance would become plain only to those with a serious intention to discover their meaning. No doubt the disciples who received an interpretation of both the parable of the Sower and the parable of the Tares were puzzled by the thought that the teaching of Jesus would neither appeal to nor persuade all who heard it. There were many adverse influences to combat it. At the conclusion of the special parable section Matthew includes a saying of Jesus which well illustrates His own approach to His hearers. A scribe "trained for the Kingdom of heaven is like a householder who brings out of his treasure what is new and what is old" (Matt. 13:52).

Although there is much that is not new in the teaching of Jesus, there is much that is unique and this takes precedence over the old.

d. *Unbelief at Nazareth.* Another incident in His own town of Nazareth occurred at this time. Although the synagogue congregation was astonished at the wisdom with which He taught, especially in view of His humble family connections, yet they were offended because of Him and they disbelieved in Him (Matt. 13:53-58; Mark 6:1-6; cf. Luke 4:16-30). Matthew records that because of this He could not perform many miracles, while Mark mentions that He healed only a "few sick people" (Mark 6:5). Jesus' own comment on this sad state of affairs was to cite a proverb about a prophet never having honor in His own country. He was clearly not surprised at the limitations imposed on His activity through man's unbelief.

e. *The Death of John the Baptist.* So far there has been little indication of the attitude of the civil authorities toward Jesus, but all the synoptic gospels mention that Jesus' fame reached the ears of Herod. It troubled Herod because rumors were spreading that John the Baptist, whom he had beheaded, was risen from the dead. It was for this reason that he desired to see Jesus. Both Matthew and Mark relate the circumstances of the beheading (Matt. 14:3 ff.; Mark 6:17 ff.). It happened in response to a malicious request by Herod's sister-in-law named Herodias, at a drunken festival at which Herodias' own daughter danced a sensuous dance. Both evangelists refer to Herod's dismay at the request for John the Baptist's head on a platter, but he had made his rash promise under oath and would not break the oath for fear of losing face with the courtiers. The whole sordid incident throws into stark relief the ignominious end of the noble forerunner of Jesus.

f. *The Feeding of the Multitude.* When the apostles returned from their preaching mission, Jesus invited them to come apart from the crowds for a time. No doubt they had much to report and some solitary place would be more conducive for this than the midst of a bustling multitude. On this occasion solitude eluded Jesus and His disciples, who were seen crossing the sea of Galilee by boat. As a result, a multitude gathered to welcome Jesus when His boat arrived at the shore, and this provided an opportunity for further extensive teaching and for a miraculous feeding of the multitude. This latter event was so remarkable that all four evangelists record it (Matt. 14:13-21; Mark 6:30-44; Luke 9:10-17; John 6:1-15). Two of the evangelists (Matthew and Mark) mention the compassion of Jesus, which must be considered the prime motive for the miracle. Another feature of the incident is the way in which the disciples were challenged to provide food for all to eat, which they were clearly incapable of doing. All the evangelists draw attention to the smallness of the food supply available (five small loaves and two fishes) and all refer to the twelve basketsfull which were left over. Mark's account is the most vivid, for he not only mentions the greenness of the grass, but also the size and arrangement of the companies into which the multitude was divided (Mark 6:39, 40). It is John, however, who brings out the significance of the event. The people who saw the miracle wanted to make Jesus king (John 6:15), but their motives were wholly materialistic and political. So alien was this to the purpose of Jesus that He was obliged to withdraw from the crowds.

A more important aspect of the incident, which John alone reveals, is the discourse of Jesus on the theme of the true bread from heaven (John 6:16 ff.). The first part of the discourse probably was given immediately after the incident of Jesus walking on the water (see next section), in the open air, but the second part clearly was delivered in the synagogue (John 6:59). The dividing line may be the point at which John introduces the murmuring Jews into his narrative (6:41).

The type of discussion which John relates must have been typical of many dialogues. It shows Jesus always taking the initiative in turning attention to spiritual issues. The Jews wanted to satisfy their curiosity as to when Jesus had arrived on the far side of the sea; then they wanted to know what work they must do to accomplish God's work; and they requested a sign as a basis of belief, citing God's gift of manna in the wilderness. To each question Jesus gives a spiritual answer: to the first, an exhortation to seek food which endures; to the second, an exhortation to believe in God's messenger, Jesus; to the third, a reminder that the bread of God is sent from heaven, not by Moses but by God Himself. This bread is then identified with Jesus Himself. This latter theme is developed in the second part of the discourse, which shows the spiritual importance of the work Jesus came to do – to give His flesh for the life of the world (John 6:51). Many of the disciples who followed Jesus found this type of teaching so perplexing and unpalatable that they withdrew from the company of Jesus. This prompted Him to challenge the Twelve. He elicited an enthusiastic expression of faith from Peter and made a prediction of Judas' betrayal (John 6:66-71).

g. *The Walking on the Water.* Reference must be made to the incident of Jesus' walking on the sea of Galilee, which is recorded by all the evangelists except Luke, immediately after the feeding of the multitudes (Matt. 14:22 ff.; Mark 6:45 ff.; John 6:16 ff.). Conditions at sea were adverse, but Jesus took command of the situation. The linking of these two miracles is not accidental, for both demonstrate power over the natural creation. In the midst of the storm Jesus brought a message of peace. The attempt of Peter to emulate Jesus by walking on the sea is related only by Matthew. It is wholly in character, as far as Peter was concerned. His impulsive action and inadequate faith are seen against the background of the Lord's mild rebuke of him. This was part of the training of the man who was to be so greatly used in the early history of the church.

h. *The Tradition of the Elders.* The encounter between Jesus and some Jerusalem scribes and Pharisees (Matt. 15:1) shows the sharp dispute which arose between them over matters of tradition. The tradition of the elders was of paramount importance to the Jews. Since it ranked equal or even superior to the written Law, it was invested with great authority. Over a long period of time its demands had increased in quantity and burdensomeness, so as to become oppressive for the serious adherents of Judaism. The system was open to abuse, and Matthew later records some severe criticism of it on the part of Jesus. It should be recognized that the intention of these traditions was to safeguard the Law for the benefit of the populace. In the present case the Pharisees were bothered about the disciples' neglect of the ritual handwashing before meals, but Jesus points out their own failure to comply with a far more fundamental demand – the Mosaic commandment to honor parents, which was nullified by Pharisaic casuistry (Matt. 15:5). He tells the people in the presence of the Pharisees that defilement is a matter of thought and not of ritual.

3. *The Period up to the Departure of Jesus for Jerusalem on His Last Journey*

a. *In a Gentile District.* After this criticism of current traditions, Jesus proceeds to the predominantly Gentile district around Tyre and Sidon, which visit is notable because of his treatment of the Syro-Phoenician woman, who came to Him on behalf of her demon-possessed daughter (Matt. 15:21 ff.; Mark 7:24 ff.). The disciples believed that a non-Jew had no right to make any demands upon Jesus, and the statement of Jesus Himself that He was sent only to "the house of Israel" (Matt. 15:24) seemed to support this view. The saying is important for it shows the limits of the main field of His mission and the reason why He did not go further afield. His response to the remarkable faith of this Gentile woman, who was prepared to beg for a dog's share if she did not qualify among the children, shows that the limits of the mission could be liberally interpreted where the need existed.

Matthew gives in summary form other healings after Jesus' return from Tyre and Sidon (Matt. 15:29 ff.), and records that the crowd glorified God. Mark tells of Jesus healing a deaf and dumb man, and says that the people were astonished beyond measure (Mark 7:31 ff.). His account includes a specific charge to silence for those who had witnessed the miracle, although the charge went unheeded (7:36). The question arises why Jesus issued such a command. Some have seen here evidence of the Messianic secret theory which has already been noted, but there is no need to embrace that theory to find an explanation of the present charge. It was never the intention of Jesus to set Himself up as a wonder-worker, and it was therefore essential that it should be known that He did not accept such a role.

b. *The Second Feeding of a Multitude.* It is at this point that Matthew and Mark relate the feeding of the four thousand (Matt. 15:32 ff.; Mark 8:1 ff.). There are many similarities with the former incident which have led some scholars to treat them as duplicate accounts of the same event. Yet there are significant differences which were obviously regarded by the evangelists as sufficient to demonstrate that there were two accounts, not one. There was a different number of people and a different supply of available food. There were also a smaller number of baskets of fragments left over.

If it be maintained that the details became enhanced in process of transmission, it would be necessary to regard this account as more primitive than the account of the feeding of the five thousand. It is difficult to see why another thousand people were added and why two less loaves and less fish were introduced, and yet five more baskets of fragments were added. Moreover, both evangelists used a different word for basket in the present account as compared with the former story. Nevertheless, if two such events actually took place, some reason must be found for the inclusion of both of them in Matthew and Mark. They both must have considered the repetition of similar incidents of some importance. Both record the specific reference by Jesus to the two events (Matt. 16:9, 10; Mark 8:19, 20). Even with the repetition the disciples had not learned their lesson, while the Pharisees were still seeking a sign from heaven. The two recorded incidents therefore emphasize not only the constantly remarkable power of Jesus, but also the obduracy of the observers who failed to interpret its message. As for the Pharisees' request for a heavenly sign, it is no wonder that this brought from Jesus a deep sigh (Mark 8:12) and a flat rejection of any other sign than that of Jonah (Matt. 16:4). It was no doubt this incident which caused Jesus to warn the disciples about the leaven of the Pharisees and Sadducees, by which He meant their teaching (Matt. 16:5-12; Mark 8:14-21).

c. *Caesarea Philippi.* One may pass by the healing of the blind man at Bethsaida, which is notable mainly because it was performed in two stages (Mark 8:22-26), and come to the highly important discussions at Caesarea Philippi (Matt. 16:13, ff.; Mark 8:27 ff.; Luke 9:18 ff.). Jesus posed the question, "Who do men say that I am?" Four general replies were given: John the Baptist, Elijah, Jeremiah, or one of the prophets, but Peter's own conception went much further. Matthew gives his testimony in its fullest form: "You are the Christ, the Son of the living God" (Matt. 16:16). Since it was from this point onward that Jesus began to concentrate on the training of the Twelve, this confession must have possessed special significance for Him. All the synoptists say that Jesus charged His disciples to tell no one about this, which reveals His awareness of the difficulties men would have in recognizing His true character.

No reasons are given why Peter and, presumably, others were led to identify Jesus so confidently with the long awaited Messiah. They had seen many evidences of His power, but many others had done the same and yet had not believed. Jesus Himself reminded Peter that He had not come to this conclusion through any human agency, but by revelation from God the Father.

It is impossible to ascertain what content was conveyed by the title "Son of the living God," but Peter was clearly recognizing some claims to deity. What such a confession meant to Jesus may be inferred from the blessing that He immediately pronounced on Peter, and from His prediction about him. When Jesus said to Peter, "on this rock I will build my church" (Matt. 16:18), it was one of the only two recorded occasions when He used the word "church" (*ekklesia;* cf. Matt. 18:17).

It is impossible to discuss here the problems which have been raised concerning this statement, but the crux of the matter is the interpretation of the word "rock." Is Peter himself intended, or is it his confession? In favor of the former is the play on Peter's name, and in favor of the latter is the teaching of other Scriptures which speak of Christ as the church's foundation. If the former is correct, it could only draw attention to the important place which Peter would occupy in the coming church, and one may recall that it was through his preaching that both the first Jews and the first Gentiles became Christians (Acts 2 and 10). Nevertheless, a church which was to withstand the gates of hell, as Jesus predicted, would need a surer foundation than the unstable Peter.

He was further given the promise of the keys of the Kingdom, which carried with it the power to bind and loose. This must be understood in conjunction with the similar injunction in Matthew 18:18, which is addressed to all the disciples. It is fitting that when Jesus turned to the training of the Twelve He first concentrated on Peter, for it was this man who immediately afterwards tried to rebuke Him for predicting His death.

That Caesarea Philippi marks a turning point in the ministry of Jesus is clear from the fact that He at once began to share with His disciples something of the dread events which He knew lay ahead. It is significant that this first prediction of the Passion was inseparably linked to the resurrection, as were the subsequent predictions.

It was not easy for the disciples to grasp the need for Jesus to suffer, and it was still harder for them to understand the place of suffering in their own lives. Self-denial is no easy lesson to learn, and it was necessary for Jesus to begin the conditioning process at this stage of the ministry to allow opportunities for much more teaching in the same vein.

d. *The Transfiguration.* The immediate sequence of events at this period is not in doubt, for all three synoptists agree on the order of events. The Transfiguration of Jesus follows the Caesarea confession, and this is followed by the healing of the epileptic boy, the second prediction of the Passion, and the dispute about greatness (cf. Matt. 17:1 ff.; Mark 9:2 ff.; Luke 9:28 ff.). In any account of the life of Jesus the Transfiguration must assume an important place because of its revelation of the glory of Jesus in a unique manner. The fact that even this revelation was seen by only three of the disciples is also significant, for it shows the existence of an inner group within the Twelve. It is not at once apparent why Jesus did not invite others to accompany Him, but the failure of the three to appreciate the meaning of the event is a sufficient indication of what would probably have been the reaction of the rest. In any case, Jesus was not to be transfigured before men as a public spectacle. Only enough witnesses were to be present to vouch for the reality of the experience.

The vision itself consisted of three stages. First, Jesus was changed so that not only His face but also His clothes radiated an extraordinary light, and there appeared with Him Moses and Elijah. Secondly, Peter makes his perfectly understandable, but thoroughly inappropriate, suggestion that some kind of dwelling booths should be constructed for the transfigured Christ and His two heavenly companions. Thirdly, a voice from the cloud urged them to concentrate on hearing Jesus because He is the beloved Son in whom God delights. The reaction of awe on the part of the disciples marks the climax of the occasion, after which Jesus resumes His normal appearance.

In assessing the place of this event in the mission of Jesus various factors must be borne in mind. It showed the true nature of Jesus, and by way of contrast helps mankind to understand more fully the meaning of His humiliation through the incarnation and subsequent Passion. This was no ordinary man. He was truly the Son of the living God, as Peter had just previously confessed. The confession, if but dimly understood when made, assumed a glorious realization for Peter as he gazed at the transfigured Christ. Neither for Peter nor for the other two did that transient glimpse of the glories of Jesus allay the appalling doubts, and, in the case of Peter, prevent the emphatic denials which were to mark their reactions to the Passion of Jesus. Their abiding grasp of the glories of Jesus was not to come this way, but by the hard experiences of His Passion leading to His resurrection.

Another factor of this event to bear in mind is the part played in it by Moses and Elijah. It is generally supposed that they represent the Law and the Prophets, to which Jesus is seen to be superior. Luke tells that they talked about the coming decease of Jesus at Jerusalem, and this must have been designed to add supernatural sanction to the prediction of His death which Jesus had made to His disciples just prior to the Transfiguration. It was not intended to be generally understood until after the resurrection, for Jesus forbids the three disciples to tell any others until then (Matt. 17:9).

The sight of Elijah in the vision raised a problem in their minds. They recalled the scribal teaching about Elijah as the forerunner of the Messiah. Perhaps they wondered why they had not seen him before, since it had now dawned upon them that Jesus was the Messiah. This opened the way for Jesus to make clear to them that John the Baptist had fulfilled the role of Elijah.

e. *More Miracles.* At the foot of the mountain another problem confronted the other disciples (Matt. 17:14 ff.; Mark 9:14 ff.; Luke 9:37 ff.). In the absence of the Master they were clearly impotent to deal with an abnormality such as an epileptic demoniac. Jesus was deeply affected by their lack of faith. The incident showed something of the caliber of the men whom Jesus was training for the future ministry of the Church. They had yet to learn how to deal with the impossible (Matt. 17:21; cf. Mark 9:23). This was a lesson which had to be repeated on other occasions (cf. Matt. 21:21; Mark 11:22; Luke 17:6). The present incident gives an example of a direct confrontation between the power of Jesus and the power of the devil, an illustration of Christ's constant struggle, which had earlier found its classic expression in the Temptation in the wilderness.

The second prediction by Jesus of His Passion and Resurrection is a natural sequel to the Transfiguration (Matt. 17:22, 23; Mark 9:30-32; Luke 9:43-45). All the synoptic writers mention the disciples' reactions. Matthew says they were distressed (Matt. 17:23), while Mark and Luke mention their lack of understanding and their hesitancy to ask Jesus for an explanation

(Mark 9:32; Luke 9:45). He found no support for His coming trials, even from His closest disciples. This was the temper of mind which caused them all finally to forsake Him during His Passion.

There are two more events which throw light on the approach of Jesus during this period. Matthew records the occasion when Peter was asked whether His master had paid the Temple tax, and he answered in the affirmative. The incident led Jesus to point out to him that only subjects of kings, not sons, are obliged to pay taxes (Matt. 17:24-27). Even in the matter of the Temple tax Jesus desired that no offense should be given, and He instructed Peter to pay the tax for himself and for Jesus from a shekel to be found in the mouth of a fish.

Many have found difficulties about this story on the grounds of the strange character of the miracle and the fact that it was performed for Jesus' own needs. Some seek a solution by attributing the story to less reliable tradition and claim it as an example of embellishment of the miraculous which took place in the tradition. The evidence does not require such a theory. The miracle is essentially of supernatural knowledge rather than a suspension of the laws of nature. It is certainly strange and indeed unexpected, but these are not sufficient factors to disprove its authenticity.

The other event is recorded by both Mark (9:38-41) and Luke (9:49-50). John reported seeing an exorcist casting out demons in Jesus' name. The disciples had forbidden him to do this because he did not belong to the group. Jesus warns them against this, for He is prepared to accept any service done in His name.

f. *More Sayings of Jesus.* Of the sayings of this period the most notable is Jesus' answer to the disciples when they were disputing about who is the greatest in the kingdom of heaven. He used a small child as an object lesson and taught by this means that humility is of the greatest importance in His Kingdom (Matt. 18:1 ff.). This is a virtue which the Greeks despised and for which the Jews were certainly not noted. In the process of training the Twelve, Jesus imparted to them a totally new code of values. They needed to learn that greatness lies along the path of service. The incident provided an occasion for Jesus to warn the disciples about causing offense to others and to give some drastic advice for dealing with the source of the offense (Matt. 18:6-9; Mark 9:42-48).

Matthew includes a striking parable to illustrate the need for forgiveness (Matt. 18:23-35). It concerned two servants of a king. One owed him a very large sum which he was unable to pay. He received full remission of the debt because of the king's mercy. The same servant was himself a creditor to the other servant who owed him a paltry sum compared with his own debt, but he treated him without mercy. The king's wrath was turned against the servant whom he had forgiven. From this story Jesus brings out the need for all to exercise forgiveness. It was told in answer to Peter's query concerning how many times a brother should be forgiven. In the kingdom of heaven there is no limit either to the number of times or to the size of the offense involved. Such forgiveness demands great largeness of heart.

7

The Closing Period

THIS IS THE most difficult period in which to arrange the narrative in any certain sequence either chronologically or geographically. Matthew and Mark are very brief, while Luke collects into a journey narrative a great deal of material which appears to be loosely linked.

1. *Moving Toward Jerusalem*

For Luke there is a sense of an inevitable movement of Jesus toward Jerusalem, subsequent to the two specific predictions of the Passion. Nevertheless, it cannot be denied that the impression of movement is slight. In one section (Luke 9:51-18:31), the references to Jerusalem are perplexing. Luke 9:51 indicates that Jesus set His face toward Jerusalem. Luke 10:38 shows Him in the village of Mary and Martha (Bethany). Luke 17:11 shows Him passing along between Samaria and Galilee on His way to Jerusalem. Luke 18:31 records His declared intention to go up to Jerusalem. Luke 18:35 ff. shows Him in the region of Jericho, and Luke 19:28 tells of His final movement toward Jerusalem and leads to the record of His entry into the city. It is difficult to fit all these references to Jerusalem into the same visit. Indeed, it is simpler to find suitable occasions for the Johannine material (John 7-10) if at least two distinct visits to Jerusalem are postulated. Even then no satisfactory chronological arrangement can be made. It may be questioned whether any advantage would accrue from such an arrangement. It is better to retain as far as possible the impressions given by Luke and to deal separately with the additional material belonging to the Jerusalem ministry related by John. For convenience, therefore, the travel narrative of Luke will be divided at the end of Luke 13 (the lament over Jerusalem) in order to record the events and discourses of John 7-10. It should be noted that whereas the greater part of the material in this section of Luke is peculiar to him, there is much that is paralleled in other contexts in Matthew and there are a few sections which are shared by all three synoptists. In the following brief survey emphasis will fall on Luke's special contribution.

a. *From Galilee to Bethany.* In none of the other gospels is Jesus' own dramatic awareness of the nearness of the climax brought out as vividly as it is in Luke's brief comment on the commencement of the final journey (Luke 9:51). The resoluteness with which Jesus faces Jerusalem is specifically marked. The first event on the journey occurred when He was about to pass through a Samaritan village (Luke 9:51-56). The direction of His face roused the opposition of the inhabitants. The desire of James and John to wreak vengeance by means of heavenly fire is remarkable for its naïve incongruity. It was not in their power to do what they suggested, and it was utterly alien to the spirit of Jesus. His path to Jerusalem was not to be strewn with burned villages as emblems of anger, but with many instances of patient forbearance toward those who had little understanding of the burden of His mission. His rebuke of the suggestion could hardly have been otherwise.

Some mission activity must still nonetheless be organized. First, the disciples needed instruction about what type of people were suitable to be followers of Christ, and Luke records Jesus' dealing with three typical examples (9:57-62). The main characteristics are a willingness to bear hardship and a persistence which would never look back. Even the apostles forsook Him during the Passion and would certainly not have been fit for the Kingdom apart from the restoring grace of God. These rigorous demands form the prelude to the sending out of the Seventy (Luke 10:1-16). There are strong similarities between the mission charge to the Seventy and the one given to the Twelve. Luke makes clear that the main purpose of the mission of the Seventy was to prepare the way in the places where Jesus was intending to visit. They were to proclaim the nearness of the Kingdom (Luke 10:9). They were in fact ambassadors for Jesus Himself (cf. Luke 10:16). In His commission Jesus adds a special denunciation of Chorazin, Bethsaida, and Capernaum, in all of which towns the spiritual significance of His mighty works had been utterly lost. No doubt this reflection of His own experience was intended to prepare the disciples for similar negative responses to their ministry.

The mission of the Seventy was presumably of short duration, for Luke tells of their return with joy soon afterward. It was their power over demons which especially elated them, but Jesus has to warn them to get their priorities right: God's estimate of them is of greater moment than their authority over demons (Luke 10:17-20). The immaturity and yet the genuineness of these men must have particularly struck Jesus at this time, for He offered a prayer of thanksgiving that revelation comes not through man's own understanding, but by the sovereign act of God (10:21, 22). As compared with others, the disciples were in a particularly privileged position (10:23, 24).

Unlike the Matthaean parables, the Lukan parables are not generally collected into groups, but they have as their setting some incident which gives them their immediate purpose. The parable of the good Samaritan is an admirable illustration of this (10:25-37). A Jewish lawyer's dialogue with Jesus concerning eternal life draws out the parable which is intended to show the practical application of what the lawyer already knew theoretically. It was one thing to pronounce love to one's neighbor as part of the divine requirement for the inheriting of eternal life; it was quite another to recognize that the term "neighbor" was so extensive that it even included Samaritans. In view of the constant animosity which existed between the Jews and Samaritans, the lawyer's astonishment at Jesus' interpretation of what being a good neighbor is can well be imagined. Moreover, the parable itself conveys more than an example. It illustrates vividly the basic principle of compassion, which was one of the most characteristic features in the life of Jesus.

By this time Jesus had arrived at Bethany, near Jerusalem (10:38-42). There is no way of knowing whether this was the first time that Jesus had visited the home of Mary and Martha. Luke's interest in the story is to show the quite different reactions of the two sisters, one revealing her devotion to Jesus by practical domestic chores, the other listening to His teaching. His commendation of the latter emphasizes the aspect of His mission which was uppermost in His mind at the time.

b. *Some Teaching on Prayer.* The disciples must often have

watched Jesus praying, and on one occasion they asked Him to teach them to pray. He gave them a pattern prayer similar to the one in the Sermon on the Mount, only more brief (11:2-4). To give them further guidance He told a parable about a persistent man who begged food from his friend at midnight and who, because of his persistence, received what he needed (11:5 ff.). This story led to Jesus' comprehensive assurances regarding prayer. The heavenly Father may be relied upon to be infinitely more considerate than human fathers, who with all their limitations would not mock their own children's earnest requests. Again, Jesus was Himself the finest example of His own teaching, for He lived in constant dependence on His Father.

c. *More Teaching by Parables.* In the remaining section of Luke where much of the material is peculiar to him, the sequence appears to be governed by alternating passages dealing with the disciples and the Pharisees. It is evidently Luke's purpose to illustrate by this means the different approach of Jesus to the two groups. It will be convenient to split Luke's material at Luke 13:35.

In response to a question about inheritance from one of the crowd surrounding Jesus at the time, He told the parable of the rich fool (12:13-21). The inheritance which he had stored up so laboriously was never enjoyed because of the man's death. This led Jesus to add a general application of the parable to warn all who have a wrong concept of riches. Following this, Luke includes a collection of sayings reminiscent of the teaching in the Sermon on the Mount. Next he relates the incident in which Pilate killed some Galileans and mixed their blood with sacrifices, and after that the calamity of the people killed by the fall of the tower of Siloam upon them (13:1-5). Such disasters obviously raise problems, but it is significant that Jesus does not give a theological or philosophical discussion of the problems involved. He used the incidents as a challenge to His hearers to repent. This challenge is strengthened by means of a parable about a fig tree which was producing no fruit and for which the vinedresser pleads that it be given one more chance with adequate watering and fertilizing (13:6-9). The parable is not applied by Jesus, but its application is clear enough. A real change of life should be evident by the fruit produced, but without such fruit the tree itself is useless.

d. *Encounters With Pharisees.* In the next section Pharisees are mainly involved, although not exclusively. It was the ruler of a synagogue who took exception to Jesus' healing, on the Sabbath day, an infirm woman, whose illness was of long standing (Luke 13:10-17). Jesus' answer was strongly worded. He condemned the hypocrisy of His opponents, who would not hesitate to care for their domestic animals on the Sabbath. It is with some relish that Luke records that His adversaries were put to shame, while the people generally rejoiced.

While Jesus was again on His way toward Jerusalem, He was accosted by some Pharisees who advised Him to flee from Herod (Luke 13:31 ff.). These Pharisees had reckoned without taking into account the fixed purpose of Jesus, which was not to be thwarted by a man like Herod, whom Jesus described as "that fox." His destiny was, in fact, in the hands of God, not Herod. It is directly subsequent to this that Luke includes the lament over Jerusalem which Matthew gives later (cf. Matt. 23:37-39). Jesus reveals both tenderness and rebuke in this lament, as He uses the vivid imagery of a hen gathering her chickens under her wings. Since He said, "How often would I have gathered your children," it seems to point to more visits to Jerusalem than the synoptists record.

e. *Jesus at Two Jewish Feasts.* Luke's story will be left at this point to consider John's account of the events which took place at the Feasts of Tabernacles and Dedication, both held at Jerusalem.

John recounts that Jesus was in Galilee just before the Feast of Tabernacles (John 7:2). His family urged Him to go to the feast for its prestige value, but they did not believe in Him and clearly misunderstood the real nature of His mission. Jesus makes clear that His time has not yet come and any open demonstration to the world would be contrary to God's timing. Throughout, Jesus was deeply conscious of working according to a divine timetable. Although He specifically avoided any public demonstration, He nevertheless went to the feast privately after His brothers had gone on ahead.

Many were looking for Him at the feast. People were privately expressing diverse opinions about Him. When He finally did show Himself, it was without ostentation, in the role of a teacher. Indeed, His skill in that role caused the Jews to marvel. This led Jesus to make some comments about the theme of authority (7:14 ff.). His own authority was from the One who sent Him, in contrast to Moses whose teaching they did not keep. The Jews raised the question of origins and dismissed any possibility of Jesus being the Messiah on the grounds that His parentage and origin were known. Jesus repeated that He came from the One who sent Him.

Teaching of this sort among the people prompted the Pharisees to take action to arrest Jesus. Officers were commissioned to do this (7:32). They overheard Jesus having a discussion with the Jews over His future destiny, which completely baffled His audience (7:33 ff.). They thought He might be referring to the dispersion. Still the officers took no action when on the last day of the feast Jesus made a public announcement about the gift of the Spirit which He would give to His disciples (7:37 ff.). He took advantage of the water ceremonial performed at the feast to illustrate a spiritual truth.

John records more specific teaching about the Holy Spirit than any of the other evangelists. The statement in the present context is important because it makes clear that the gift of the Spirit depends on and consequently follows the glorifying of Jesus (7:39).

Such teaching as this only further baffled the hearers and caused a dispute as to whether or not Jesus could possibly be the Christ. His Galilean connections caused difficulties (7:41). The same problem was raised again, when the Pharisees discussed the matter at the highest level following the return of their officers without arresting Jesus. They had been deeply impressed by His teaching (7:46). At the council the attitude of Nicodemus is interesting in the light of his earlier interview with Jesus. He issues a mild rebuke to those who wish to condemn Him without a hearing. In this incident the attitude of the Pharisees fully agrees with that recorded in the synoptic gospels.

There followed further discussions with the Jews, mainly about the testimony of Jesus to Himself (8:12 ff.). When He claimed to be the Light of the world, the Pharisees asserted that self-testimony of this kind cannot be true. The whole dispute focuses attention on the difficulties which confronted Jesus in expressing concepts which were foreign to the way of thinking of the religious leaders of His day. It was unintelligible to them when Jesus claimed the testimony of the Father in support of Him. To them the Father was known only through the Law, not through Jesus. He had to remind them that the nature of His authority would be understood only when the Son of Man had been lifted up (8:28).

The conversation next turns to Abraham and the relation of the Pharisees to him (John 8:39 ff.). When Jesus spoke of freedom, even the Jews who had believed in Him protested. The promise of freedom implies the absence of it and no son of Abraham could ever conceive of himself as a slave. It is not surprising that the discussion became rather bitter, with the Jews actually maintaining that Jesus was demon-possessed (8:48). This incident shows Jesus confronted with the national pride of the Jewish people in their connection with Abraham, but He points out that racial connections need to be supported by deeds worthy of Abraham. The inconsistency of the position of His accusers led Jesus to the astonishing charge that they were of their father the devil (8:44).

The strength of the conflict in which Jesus was engaged is vividly seen. The accusers still cannot get away from the Abraham theme, for they challenge Jesus to say whether He is greater than Abraham (8:53), and again He appeals to the testimony of the Father. He even maintains that Abraham rejoiced to see His day (8:56), and that He was in existence before Abraham. The immediate reaction of the Jews is not left to imagination. John concisely reports that they took up stones to stone Him, but that Jesus hid Himself from them.

John's account of the healing by Jesus of a man born blind and the subsequent encounter of the man with the Pharisees is dramatically told (ch. 9). There are several features in this incident which call for special comment. The disciples were bothered about the explanation of man's calamity, but Jesus does not offer any assistance in answering the theological problem. He is concerned about what will bring most glory to God. Moreover, He makes clear that His proposed action is inextricably bound up with His mission as the Light of the world. The application of the mission is twofold, for not only was the man's physical sight restored by Jesus, but through this event his spiritual perception was also sharpened.

John traces the growth of the man's faith as he disputes with the Pharisees. Every conceivable reason was advanced for disbelieving the reality of the miracle, but the man himself asserted his own personal experience, which could not be gainsaid. As a result of his bold testimony, he was cast out of the synagogue.

Knowledge of this having come to Jesus, He sought him out in order to challenge him regarding his faith. The confession which this drew from the man forms the climax of the story. With restored physical sight and awakened spiritual insight, he contrasts strongly with the Pharisees who constantly demonstrated their blindness, although they were not aware of it.

Following this, John records further teaching of Jesus concerning Himself, this time under the imagery of a shepherd (ch. 10). The illustration from the sheepfold would have been familiar to His hearers. The shepherd's care to protect the sheep, the sharp distinction between the real shepherd and the man hired to do the job who had no interest in the welfare of the sheep, the intimate relationship between the shepherd and each individual sheep, and the picture of the shepherd leading out his flock to pasture would all have been well-known features of the contemporary pastoral scene. But they did not understand the implications of what Jesus was illustrating (10:6). Because of this, Jesus adds some further comments, the most important of which is that the good Shepherd lays down His life for the sheep (10:11, 15). The voluntary character of this act is particularly stressed (10:18).

Another important factor is that Jesus distinguishes between folds and flocks. Not all belong to the same fold, but all belong to the same flock (10:16) This seems to be a pointed reminder that the Jews were not the only group of people with a claim upon the good Shepherd's care.

Once again the teaching of Jesus evoked the charge of demon possession from some of the Jews, but others were not convinced of this in view of the character of the sayings and the miraculous healing of the blind man.

Similar teaching was given by Jesus at the Feast of Dedication held in winter time. Some of the Jews wanted Jesus to state plainly whether or not He was the Messiah, and Jesus rebukes them for not believing. The reason for their unbelief, he says, was that they did "not belong to the sheep" (10:26). The security of Christ's sheep is nothing less than the security of the good Shepherd's hand. On this occasion the opposition to Him was more violent. They took up stones to stone Him. In spite of the ugliness of the situation, Jesus shows Himself in command by attempting to reason with the Jews. His appeal to them was based on Scripture, which, He says, cannot be broken (10:35).

Significantly, Jesus urges them to believe His works if they cannot believe His words. Once again they tried without success to arrest Him (10:39).

At this point Jesus goes again to trans-Jordan (10:40); this will be a convenient place to return to Luke's travel narrative, which is also much concerned with Jesus' clash with Pharisees.

f. *Jesus Dines With Pharisees* (Luke 14). It must often have happened that Jesus was offered hospitality in a home, though no doubt infrequently at the home of a Pharisee. One may be grateful to Luke for recording a sequence of events and discussions which occurred during such a meal (14:1 ff.). Lawyers and Pharisees were on the watch to see what Jesus would do, since it was the Sabbath. They were anticipating that He might contravene the Jewish Law. He knew what was in their minds, for before healing a man with dropsy He addressed His observers with a question about the lawfulness of healing on the Sabbath day. No answer was given; which was a silent testimony to their embarrassment.

Luke next records a parable which was especially designed for the guests of the dinner (Luke 14:7 ff.). Jesus had noted their eagerness to choose the chief seats and reminded them that it was humble people who would be exalted. This led to an exhortation urging hospitality for poor and unfortunate people, which reflects the social attitude of Jesus. His deep compassion was in marked contrast to the Pharisaic quibbles over Sabbath procedure, to the detriment of individual welfare.

One of the Pharisees ventured to draw attention to the blessedness of eating bread in the Kingdom (14:15 ff.), but again Jesus detected a misunderstanding. He told another parable, one about some people who made excuses when invited to a banquet. The excuses appeared legitimate enough, but they showed a discourteous attitude to the hosts. The point of the story is seen in the sequel. The social outcasts were to be invited instead, a fact which adds further emphasis to the social consciousness of Jesus. In this He differed strongly from most of the Pharisees.

g. *Address to the Multitudes.* Jesus was once more followed by great multitudes and turned to address them on the subject of the cost of discipleship (14:25-35). This in itself was not a new theme, for it had been mentioned before, just after the confession at Caesarea Philippi (cf. 9:23). Here, however, it is elaborated. Discipleship involves some testing of priorities.

Jesus speaks of the need for hating one's own family connections, but the idea of hating in this context must be regarded as relative. It is a question of wholehearted committal to the cause of Christ. Jesus illustrates His meaning by saying that no one puts in a foundation without estimating the cost of the whole house, or goes to war against a well-organized and powerful enemy without weighing the possibilities of carrying the campaign through to success. That is simple human prudence.

The same principle of forethought should apply to Christian discipleship. It demands wholehearted renunciation, and those not willing for so great a cost would be well-advised to make no start. Disciples who begin and then lose their effectiveness are like salt which has lost its taste and hence becomes good for nothing. In this simile Jesus was using a Jewish proverb.

h. *Further Parables for the Pharisees*. Pharisaism had no message for sinners and little sympathy for those who were concerned about them. In their eyes sinners and tax collectors were outcasts of society. No wonder, therefore, that they regarded with contempt anyone who actually sat down to a meal with them. It was common knowledge that Jesus shared their hospitality, and when the Pharisees and scribes saw that Jesus had so large a following among these outcasts, they murmured against Him in His hearing.

This brought from Jesus a sequence of three parables to illustrate God's attitude toward those who were being officially treated as lost, for whom Pharisaism held out no hope (ch. 15). These parables are essentially parables of restoration. A shepherd restores his lost sheep to the fold, a woman restores a lost coin to her treasure store, and a father restores a wayward son to the family circle. In all of the parables the element of joy is emphasized; in the first two, there is joy in heaven over restored sinners; in the third, joy is an expression of the father's feelings when his son returns.

The application of the parables to the Pharisees is clear enough. They did not even desire the restoration of sinners, let alone show any inclination to rejoice over the possibility. There is no doubt that their murmuring, which formed the setting for the parables, finds a distinctive echo in the attitude of the elder brother in the third parable, who objected to the rejoicing over a brother who had lived so utterly irresponsibly. This elder brother was a typical Pharisee, more concerned about his own loyal achievements than about the miserable state of his brother, and more anxious to condemn than to forgive.

The vividness of the parables in their portrayal of human sentiments throws further light on the human insight and sympathy of Jesus. He was ever more concerned with the uplift of human lives than with those who considered themselves to be too superior to stir a finger to help the needy.

i. *Teaching for the Disciples.* The next brief section (16:1-13) is addressed to the disciples (understood in the widest sense of a group of generally interested people), and takes the form of a parable with comments upon it. It was a story about an unjust steward who had wasted his master's possessions and had been informed that as a consequence he would lose his job. He makes provision for the emergency by giving considerable discounts to those who owed money to his master, with a view to winning their friendship which would stand him in good stead for the future. The action itself appears dishonest, but the master recognized the man's prudence. Presumably the steward, until actually dismissed, had powers to remit portions of debts, and the master did not condemn him on this account. The parable, therefore, illustrates prudence for selfish ends, without regard for moral principles.

Jesus recommends the disciples to make friends by means of unrighteous mammon. Does this mean that Jesus is condoning an unprincipled approach? It may at first sight appear so, but it must be kept in mind that the details of the parable should not be pressed. The major purpose is to urge greater wisdom on the part of disciples than was evident among unprincipled men. On purely materialistic principles, unrighteous mammon is man's only means of security.

Jesus proceeded to contrast with this unrighteous mammon true riches. Faithfulness in using the one is the test for the using of the other. Unrighteous mammon is therefore to be regarded as no more than a means to an end. No one can serve both mammon and God. This section of the teaching of Jesus illuminates His own attitude toward materialistic things. He did not ignore their usefulness, but demanded their subservience to God.

j. *Another Clash With the Pharisees.* The preceding parable fell on some Pharisaic ears and caused scoffing at Jesus' attitude to money (16:14 ff.). Jesus not only insisted that God's judgments are based on knowledge of the heart, and not on outward appearances, but also He told a parable to show how unreliable a guide material wealth can be (16:19 ff.). A contrast is made between a poor man, who was afflicted with disease, and a rich man, at whose gate the poor man had sat and begged. The rich man went to Hades, and the poor man to Abraham's bosom, with a fixed chasm between them. There follows a conversation between the rich man in Hades and Abraham, with whom he pleads in vain for some relief. Abraham says that even if it were possible for Lazarus to return to earth to warn the rich man's relatives, he would not be believed any more than Moses, whose teaching they already possessed but did not heed.

The Pharisees, with their love of money, would see the point of the challenge. The rich man's plight was not because he was rich, but because of his failure to use his riches to alleviate the needs of others, while indulging in luxuries for himself.

k. *The Apostles Receive Teaching About Service.* Jesus now appeals to common procedure in the employment of servants (17:5-11). If a servant's job is to do both agricultural and domestic work, he would not expect to be thanked if his master called him in from the field and asked him to serve him at table. He would only be performing his duty. In the same way, no one can ever say that he has done more than his duty to God, for even after doing all that is commanded of him, he has done only what is his duty. If this teaching was overheard by the Pharisees, they must have been astonished at such a statement. The idea of reward loomed large in their system and they believed that merit could be stored up in heaven. Jesus' teaching was diametrically opposed to theirs.

l. *The Healing of the Lepers.* Luke again draws attention to the fact that Jesus was approaching Jerusalem and then introduces an event which happened in the vicinity of Samaria (17:11 ff.). Ten lepers, begging for mercy, met Jesus who commanded them to show themselves to the priests; and as they went they were healed. They must have acted in faith that healing would be given. This was not the main feature of the incident, for when they discovered that they were healed, only one returned to give thanks to Jesus, and he was a Samaritan. Jesus particularly points out the fact that only a "stranger" returns (17:18). The whole incident shows not only the compassion of Jesus but the universal scope of His mission. The story is probably intended to illustrate the ingratitude which was characteristic of the Jewish nation in response to the merciful acts of God.

m. *Sayings About the Kingdom and About the Future.* A question put by the Pharisees about the Kingdom drew from Jesus a statement that the Kingdom was in their midst or was within them (17:20 ff.). This would directly counteract any materialistic concept of the Kingdom as it was currently held among the Jews (see the chapter on "The Teaching of Jesus").

Luke then records some teaching of Jesus addressed to the disciples (17:22 ff.) on the subject of the days of the Son of man. There would be false claims that these days were near, and of these they must beware. To give them indication of the timing of those days would be as impossible as tracking lightning across the sky. Before they can come, however, the Son of man must first be rejected. The consciousness of the nearness of that event must have been strong in the mind of Jesus. There are, moreover, certain Old Testament events from the times of Noah and Lot which serve as a pattern of the times preceding the coming of the Messiah. In both cases the masses of people were totally unprepared for the divine judgment which came to them. In view of this, Jesus warns about the sharp division among men which the coming of the Son of man will create.

n. *Two Parables About Prayer.* Luke includes two parables presumably addressed to the disciples, which possess certain features in common, and which deal with different aspects of prayer (18:1-18). The first, the parable of the unjust judge, commends constancy in prayer, and the second, the parable of the Pharisee and the tax-collector, commends humility. The first provides an example of unrighteousness, the second of self-righteousness. In the first parable the judge is portrayed in the worst possible light, as a man who had no thought of God and no respect for man. The impression is at once created that justice is impossible from such a man, and this impression is deepened by the description of the plaintiff as a poor widow who had no one to protect her against an adversary. The judge gave in, not because he cared for justice, but because of the continual requests of the widow and to have refused would have caused him more embarrassment than to yield. The focus of the parable is on the power of constant petition, not on the character of the judge.

When Jesus applies the parable He argues from the lesser to

the greater. What a rascally unrighteous man will do is nothing compared with what may be expected from a righteous God. Jesus leads up to an exhortation to His hearers that such constancy of faith, as was exemplified by the persistent widow, might be found when He returns.

The other parable presents in strong contrast the attitude of a self-righteous Pharisee and the attitude of a man whom the Pharisees despised – a tax-collector. Both are represented as praying in the Temple, but the Pharisee is more conscious of himself and of his own superiority over others than he is of God. Consequently, his prayer is regarded as ineffective. The tax collector, overwhelmed with a deep sense of his own need, can do no more than cry to God for mercy. The egotism of the Pharisee may have been heightened to emphasize the contrast between these two men, but there is enough evidence to prove that self-righteousness was an accepted characteristic among the Pharisaic party. No Pharisee would readily have admitted that his achievements were useless in his approach to God, for his whole religious life centered around what he himself could do in the pursuit of piety. How very distasteful such attitudes must have been to Jesus is suggested by His warm commendation of the opposite quality, humility.

At this point Luke returns to material which is shared by the other synoptic gospels, and these two parables may be said to terminate His special travel narrative. Before starting the final journey to Jerusalem, it will be necessary to include the account of the raising of Lazarus at Bethany and to consider the consequences (John 11).

o. *The Raising of Lazarus.* This is unquestionably the most astonishing of all the miracles performed by Jesus. It is the climax of John's Book of Signs and sets out the humanity as well as the deity of Jesus (11:1 ff.). The bare details may be stated in few words. Lazarus dies in Bethany. Jesus is in Trans-Jordan, but although He knows about the illness of Lazarus, He delays His visit to Bethany until it is too late to find him alive. His sisters, Mary and Martha, who have already been introduced earlier through Luke's account, are convinced that had Jesus arrived soon enough He would have prevented their brother's death, but they do not show faith enough to believe that He could or would raise Lazarus from the dead. Jesus was deeply moved at the scene and wept, but He coupled with this human emotion the tremendous power of divine authority as Lazarus is commanded to come out of the grave.

What distinguishes this story from a narrative of sheer wonder-working power are the deep personal reactions which are faithfully reported. There are: the fear of the disciples to go to Judaea, followed by their rash resolve to die with Jesus; the different reactions of Martha and Mary, the former more outspoken than the latter; the comment of the Jews when they saw Jesus weeping; and the reaction of the Pharisees and the chief priests in renewing their plans to kill Jesus.

When John records this stupendous miracle, he does so with a spiritual objective. It is part of his testimony to lead people to believe that Jesus is the Christ, the Son of God. If this incident is true, then Jesus immediately is seen to have unique power. However conceivable it might be to explain away some of the other miracles, it is impossible in this case. It is a foreshadowing of the far greater event of the resurrection of Christ.

Throughout the incident Jesus took advantage of the opportunity to impart teaching so that the significance of the miracle might be understood. He told the disciples that Lazarus' illness was for God's glory (11:4). When He made known to them that Lazarus was dead, He explained that the delay in His coming to Bethany was to assist them to believe (11:5). When Martha discussed the resurrection with Jesus, He declared, "I am the resurrection, and the life" (11:25), connecting the whole matter of life and death with His person. This led to a definite affirmation of faith on her part, expressed in the same terms as John stated the purpose of his entire gospel (11:27). Just prior to the miracle, Martha was assured that she was about to see the glory of God if she believed.

John pays special attention to the Pharisees' reaction. They were worried about the probable impact of the signs upon the common people, particularly if it led to any action by the occupying Roman forces. It was Caiaphas the Sadducee who gave the official opinion of the hierarchy (11:49). John states that he was the high priest during that fateful year, in commenting on Caiaphas' statement that it was more fitting for one person to die for the nation than that the whole nation should perish. The statement was more prophetic than Caiaphas realized, as John points out. Moreover, its application was also more universal than he realized, for Jesus was to die to gather many people into one family of God.

Because of the decision of the Sanhedrin to seek His death, Jesus withdrew for a time to Ephraim (11:54) and remained there until the approach of the Passover season, at which point the synoptic and Johannine narratives coalesce.

2. *The Journey Into Jerusalem*

Jesus is now in the region of Perea from where He proceeded toward Jerusalem by way of Jericho and Bethany. Various incidents took place and discourses were given before He arrived in Jericho.

a. *Conclusion of the Ministry in Perea.* The Pharisees were still pursuing Jesus, trying to trap Him with difficult questions. This must have happened frequently during this period, but both Matthew (19:1-12) and Mark (10:1-12) record a particular question that Jesus was asked about divorce. The subject had already been touched upon in the Sermon on the Mount. Here it was a question based on the teaching of the Law. Jesus shows that Moses allowed divorce only because of the hardness of peoples' hearts, although the creation ordinances presupposed a permanent union between husband and wife. By appealing to the basic principles of the Law, Jesus silenced His critics. The whole question of divorce was currently a disputed issue within the Pharisaic party itself. (See the chapter on "The Background to the Life of Jesus"). One school under Hillel took a much more liberal attitude toward it than the other under Shammai. It is clear that the approach of Jesus is nearer the latter than the former. Some of the disciples objected to the stringency of the teaching of Jesus, but He reminded them that not all could receive such teaching.

Next comes a charming interlude which shows Jesus in another role (Matt. 19:13 ff.; Mark 10:13 ff.; Luke 18:15 ff.) Little children were brought to Him for His blessing, but the disciples rebuked those who brought them. Jesus, in turn, rebuked the disciples, telling them that children were not to be hindered from coming to Him, and He used them as an example of true discipleship. The Kingdom of God, He said, must be received as a little child, a principle which would not have been readily appreciated in the first century world. Humility was not a virtue admired by either Jews or Greeks, the latter, in fact, despising it.

A rich young ruler now comes to Jesus and asks Him about eternal life (Matt. 19:16 ff.; Mark 10:17 ff.; Luke 18:18 ff.). The questioner is a pious man, for he claims to have kept the commandments from his youth. There is no necessity to question his sincerity, for Jesus does not challenge him on this account. Jesus recognized that riches were his stumbling block, which led to the suggestion that he should sell his possessions to give to the poor. The young man refused and went away sorrowful.

Since riches could be such an obstacle, Jesus makes some general comments on the danger of riches and goes on to tell a parable which had a bearing on this theme. He acknowledged that wealthy men would find it more difficult than poor men to enter the Kingdom, but He made it clear that it was not impossible for them to do so with the help of God. One of the requirements of the Kingdom was to put the interests of Christ before everything else, even before one's closest family connections.

The parable of the workers in the vineyard, which is related only in Matthew (20:1 ff.), is intended to illustrate the justice of God. Those who worked for only a small part of the day received the same pay as those who had done a full day's work. When the latter complained, they were reminded that the terms of their contract had been fulfilled. It was not that they had received less, but that the others had received proportionately more. The parable is not a pattern for industrial relationships, but an illustration of the right of the owner of the vineyard to do what he chooses. So Jesus taught the sovereignty of God.

At this point, as they drew nearer to Jerusalem, Jesus addressed Himself to the Twelve. He reminded them for the third time that He was going up to Jerusalem to be killed, even to be crucified (Matt. 20:17 ff.; Mark 10:32 ff.; Luke 18:31 ff.). This brief mention of His death highlights the severe loneliness of Jesus in His mission, for Luke comments that the disciples had no understanding of what He said (Luke 18:34). His mind must have been disturbed by the knowledge that there was rivalry among the disciples over who was to be the greatest in the coming Kingdom, and especially over the request of James and John for preferential treatment. When Jesus challenged the two about their ability to drink His cup, He alone knew the bitter experiences that were involved. The other ten were just as bad, for they could not refrain from anger at the audacity of the two. In spite of what Jesus had already said about humility, they had not learned the lesson that the greatest in the Kingdom is he who serves most. Matthew attributes the ambition of James and John to their mother, who makes the request, but Mark shows that the responsibility rested equally upon them (cf. Matt. 20:20; Mark 10:35 ff.).

The most significant feature of this incident is the statement of Jesus' own purpose in terms of service – to give His life a ransom for many (Matt. 20:28; Mark 10:45). During this period His thoughts must often have been on the essential meaning of His mission. Among those whose thoughts were so dominated by ambition to lord it over others, His own principle of sacrificial service stood out in strong contrast.

b. *In Jericho.* It is not without some point that all the synoptists relate a healing of the blind at this stage in the ministry (Matt. 20:29 ff.; Mark 10:46 ff.; Luke 18:35 ff.). The result of this brought not only light to blinded eyes but rejoicing to the multitudes. It was a welcome contrast to the quibbling of the disciples. There are some differences in the narratives which cannot be fully discussed. Matthew refers to two blind men, Mark and Luke to one; while Matthew and Luke differ in their placing of the incident. It seems clear that there were two men healed, of whom Mark and Luke select only one, and it seems equally clear that the incident happened on the outskirts of Jericho, somewhere between the old and the new Jericho.

Luke alone recounts the meeting of Jesus with Zacchaeus in Jericho (Luke 19:1-10). This again throws into bold relief the purpose of Jesus – to seek out and to save the lost (19:10). The Savior's consciousness of His immediate task thus finds opportunity to bring a challenge to a despised class of men, i.e., tax-collectors. The social effects of the Gospel are vividly seen in the immediate restitution which Zacchaeus made to those whom he had wronged. Something of the tremendous achievements of the mission of Jesus are therefore visible in token form immediately prior to the final entry into Jerusalem.

A parable recorded in Luke's gospel is especially fitting as a prelude to the entry into Jerusalem (19:11 ff.). It was told to correct the mistaken impression that the establishing of the Kingdom was imminent. A nobleman about to go away to receive a kingdom commits money to his servants with the command that they trade with it. While he is away the citizens reject the nobleman as king, and when he returns he requires each servant to give account of his trading. Responsibility is apportioned according to the results obtained. The parable ends with a statement that the nobleman's enemies were to be destroyed. It must have been in the mind of Jesus as He approached Jerusalem that its people would reject Him as king, and He knew that this would be a shock to the disciples. The recognition of faithful service during this period of rejection was essential for them to realize at this time, although they did not then fully appreciate its significance. The destruction of the enemies (if Jerusalem was in mind) took place some forty years later under the Roman siege.

c. *Jesus at Bethany.* It was six days before the Passover. The mind of Jesus is more than ever on His approaching Passion, and He seeks retreat at Bethany with Mary, Martha and Lazarus. While seated at supper, Jesus is anointed by Mary with precious ointment (John 12:1 ff.). The act was viewed differently by different people. The attitude of Jesus is strongly contrasted with that of Judas, to whom it was sheer waste. To Jesus it was an act which showed some understanding of His spiritual mission and its involvement. Mary had seized what Jesus knew was to be her last opportunity to show her identification with Him. In Jesus' mind she had prepared for His burial, and no cost was too great for that. The sense of inevitability of the coming events cannot be erased from the record. Both Matthew and Mark preserve the promise of Jesus that the woman's act would be remembered wherever the Gospel was preached.

As if to prepare still further for the doom awaiting Jesus in Jerusalem, John mentions that the Jews now proceeded to add the further intention of killing Lazarus to the earlier decision to kill Jesus (John 12:10). Nothing could bring out more vividly the appalling spiritual blindness of the Jewish national leaders.

3. *The Ministry in Jerusalem*

The preceding events have all prepared for the concluding events in Jerusalem. The hour of the Messiah has come. He had arrived only to be rejected by the leaders of His people. The point of entry is therefore the beginning of the end. But the real significance of it came to the disciples only later when they were more able to see these closing events as a whole.

a. *The Entry Into Jerusalem and the Cleansing of the Temple.* The fact that all four gospels relate the triumphal entry of Jesus into Jerusalem shows the importance which must be attached to it (Matt. 21:1-9; Mark 11:1-10; Luke 19:28-38; John 12:12 ff.). In view of the forebodings which Jesus had from time to time revealed, the manner of His entry is unexpected. From the acclamation of the multitude it would not have appeared evident that Jesus was riding into the city to be crucified within a few days. All the gospels have prepared the reader to consider more fully the attitude of Jesus than the attitude of the multitude. Matthew and John mention the fulfillment of a prophecy as if to account for the strange paradox (Matt. 21:5; John 12:15). In this way both draw attention to an important element in the consciousness of Jesus at this time – the testimony of Scripture. The royal nature of the entry is stressed in all the accounts and is clearly meant to provide a backdrop against which the somber events of the Passion might be described. As in the preceding parable (Luke 19:11-27), Jesus had come to take up His Kingdom, but not in the manner of earthly kings. The impression of triumph created by the entry is introduced only to be quickly dispelled.

As Jesus drew near, He wept over the city and predicted its doom (19:41).

According to Matthew, the first action of Jesus in Jerusalem was to cleanse the Temple (21:10 ff.), but Mark's more detailed narrative requires the prior cursing of the fig tree (Mark 11:12 ff.). The two events are not unrelated in their significance; both have a symbolic meaning for the Jewish nation.

The fig tree was impressive because of its leaves, which that year appeared earlier than usual for the time of year. It caught the eyes of Jesus who supposed that the first figs, which normally appear before the leaves, should have been on the tree. On finding none, Jesus cursed the tree. According to Mark, it was not until the next day that the disciples noticed that the tree had suddenly withered. They drew the attention of Jesus to this fact, revealing in doing so that to them it was no more than a marvel, although He, no doubt, intended it to be symbolic of Israel. The nation had all the external appearance of flourishing religiously, but had not produced the fruits of righteousness. The destruction of the tree was an illustration of God's judgment on Israel. Jesus knew, as the disciples did not, that that judgment was not far distant, as far as Jerusalem was concerned.

The drastic action of Jesus in casting out the moneychangers from the Temple is also symbolic. It was the practice for these people to exchange other currencies for the Temple currency, in which money alone the Temple tax could be paid. This enabled the unscrupulous to charge more than was due, and the same applied to the sellers of pigeons. It was no wonder that Jesus' wrath was kindled against them. His act of righteous indignation was representative of the revulsion of perfect goodness at the sight of all injustice, especially in the name of, and in the central place of, the worship of God. All the synoptic gospels record the quotation from the Scriptures made by Jesus in justification of His action. What was intended as a house of prayer had become a den of thieves. It was a symbol of what had happened to Israel as a whole. Judgment would come to it as surely as it had come to the Temple. The evangelists report various reactions to what Jesus had done. Children cried out in the Temple, "Hosanna to the Son of David"; the multitude was astonished; at the same time the chief priests and scribes intensified their determination to kill Jesus. Such a cross section of reactions was also representative of the nation as a whole.

b. *Days of Controversy*. During the closing days in Jerusalem one of the marked features was the number of conflicts which Jesus had with religious leaders and others. The priests, scribes and elders debated with Him the question of authority, but He countered with a challenge on the problem of the authority of John the Baptist (Matt. 21:23 ff.; Mark 11:27; Luke 20:1 ff.). This led to the relating of the parable about the wicked husbandmen (Matt. 21:33 ff.; Mark 12:1 ff.; Luke 20:9 ff.), which again focuses upon divine judgment on those who have wrongly used their office in the vineyard of Israel, particularly in the killing of the heir. Nevertheless, Jesus assures His hearers that the Stone which the builders rejected (i.e., Himself) would become the cornerstone of God's building.

The next controversy concerned tribute money to Caesar (Matt. 22:15 ff.; Mark 12:13 ff.; Luke 20:20 ff.). In this case the Pharisees joined with the Herodians, whom they usually avoided through dislike of their policy, to attempt to ensnare Jesus. By using a simple coin with the image of Caesar on it, He appealed to the testimony of the currency that the Jews were a subservient people, which was intensely unpalatable to the Pharisees, but nevertheless true. All the synoptists note that the opponents marveled at the answer of Jesus. Were they truly challenged to render to God what belonged to Him?

Following this, the Sadducees asked a question about the resurrection, but they fared no better (Matt. 22:23 ff.; Mark 12:18 ff.; Luke 20:27 ff.). Jesus showed that their problem about marriage in heaven displayed a misunderstanding of the spiritual nature of the resurrection. Matthew reports astonishment from the multitude; and Luke commendation from certain scribes. The masterly wisdom of Jesus made the "catch" questions put to Him look foolish, but the various hostile parties came back for more exposure from Him. A Pharisaic lawyer tried out the problem of the greatest commandment (Matt. 22:34 ff.). This was a stock question which Jesus had earlier illustrated by the parable of the good Samaritan.

Jesus Himself now put a question to the Pharisees about the lineage of the Messiah and the interpretation of Psalm 110:1. He confounded them on a matter of exegesis over which they especially prided themselves (Matt. 22:41 ff.). If the Messiah was the Son of David how could David also call him Lord? Although all the synoptists record the question, it is Matthew alone who comments that no one was able to answer Him. This is not surprising, for the hearers had no concept of the two natures of the Messiah, i.e., human and divine.

All the quibbling of the Jewish religious leaders led Jesus to denounce in strong terms the abuses of the scribes and Pharisees (Matt. 23). He does not condemn their allegiance to the Law, but their abuse of their position as teachers. Some have thought that His criticisms of these religious leaders was undeserved. It must be said, however, that although there was undoubtedly much good in Judaism, the burdens imposed on the common people had become intolerable, and much supposed piety was marred by inconsistency and hypocrisy.

The language of denunciation as reported in Matthew 23 is strongly expressed. Jesus first points out the love of ostentation among the Pharisees. Their good deeds are done in public to be seen of men. They love places of honor. They delight in receiving titles of respect from men. This kind of attitude is foreign to that of Jesus, who maintains again that those who humble themselves will be exalted and those who exalt themselves will be humbled. There was need for a reversal of current Pharisaic values. Several times in the course of the denunciation Jesus calls them hypocrites, which is a word having the force of play-acting. They were not what they appeared to be. Even their great proselytizing activity did no more than add others who were no better than themselves. Moreover, they are described as blind guides, incapable of discernment. Their petty rules about oaths illustrate the point. They cannot differentiate between important and unimportant matters: they strain out gnats and swallow camels (Matt. 23:24).

Other features which came in for heavy criticism from Jesus were their burdensome ritual requirements and their opposition to God's true messengers. In connection with the first, an example is cited from their interpretation of ritual cleansing. The outside of the cup is to be cleansed at all costs, but the inside is neglected, said Jesus, by which He meant that external adherence to cleansing regulations was useless unless it was accompanied by spiritual renewal. Another illustration which Jesus turned against them was their practice of whitewashing sepulchres so that men might see them and avoid defiling themselves by walking over them. He likened the sepulchres to their hearts, and the whitewashing to their outward show of piety. He further criticized them for outwardly honoring the prophets and yet inwardly being of the same spiritual outlook as their fathers who murdered the prophets. All through the comments of Jesus upon the scribes and Pharisees runs the same theme – they professed one thing and did another.

It is not to be supposed that every Pharisee was guilty of all the abuses that Jesus mentioned, nor may it even be supposed that these abuses were generally typical. Jesus saw the logical results of the tendencies which a legalistic system must produce, and by exposing these results He aimed to warn men against them.

It is fitting that after such denunciation of the scribes and Pharisees Jesus should once again lament over Jerusalem. Moreover, an incident which He observed at the Temple treasury served by way of contrast to illustrate His own concept of true piety. It was not the many rich men giving their large sums, but a poor widow giving a humble gift who was commended by Him (Mark 12:41 ff.).

There were, however, some sincere inquirers who came to Him, for John records the quest of some Greeks who sought Him (John 12:20 ff.), which led Jesus to speak to them about His hour of glorification. Once again attention is drawn to the thoughts uppermost in the mind of Jesus on the eve of His Passion. He thinks of Himself as a grain of wheat which must die to reproduce itself and prays that God's name may be glorified through Him. To mark the critical character of this occasion, the Father's voice is heard from heaven, saying that He had glorified it and would glorify it again, but the crowd did not understand. John, indeed, mentions that those who had seen many signs did not believe in Him (John 12:37). At the same time Jesus states that their disbelief is not merely in Him but in the Father.

c. *Words About the Future.* As His own hour draws near, Jesus instructs His disciples about future happenings. All the synoptists record parts of this eschatological teaching (Matt. 24, 25; Mark 13; Luke 21:5-38). The discourse was occasioned by the disciples' admiration for the Temple buildings, causing Jesus to predict its destruction. When this raised curiosity among them, Jesus unfolded some of the events which must happen in the future – false Christs, wars among the nations, and natural calamities. Then He predicted persecutions in store for the disciples, desolations in Judea, the rise of false teachers, celestial signs, and the coming of the Son of man. No one could know the date of this coming, but a description of it is included, couched in apocalyptic terms. Of more importance than the details of the coming is the present attitude of the disciples. The exhortation to watch and pray is essentially practical. A definite moral challenge is provided by the thought that life must be lived in the light of that coming. In the teaching of Jesus eschatology is never removed from ethical implications.

More will be said about the future aspects of the Kingdom when the teaching of Jesus is separately considered, but it is worth noting here that He did not hesitate to use apocalyptic language to express His meaning. This does not require us to think that He shared much in common with the apocalyptists. Their approach was largely pessimistic. They were visionaries whose hopes were based on insecure foundations. They testify, however, to earnest aspirations which the Christian Gospel was able to fulfill in an infinitely better way than they were able to conceive. The eschatological teaching of Jesus centers upon the coming triumph of the Son of man.

In Matthew's account of the discourse three parables are included – the ten virgins, the talents, and the sheep and the goats — all of which also contain practical implications. The wise virgins who took oil in their lamps while they waited for the bridegroom to come are commended for their preparedness, but the sorry outcome for those who did not take oil and who were not ready for the bridegroom is intended as a solemn warning. In the parable of the talents, the men who used their resources to gain other talents for their master are commended for their faithfulness, whether their gains were large or small. It was the man who did nothing, and was therefore unfaithful, who was condemned. In the third parable, it is the need of others which is the focus of attention. The sheep are those who cared for others, the goats those who did not. The former are commended, but the latter are condemned. All three parables bring out the sharp distinctions which arise in connection with the Kingdom.

4. *The Passion and Resurrection of Jesus*

a. *From the Plot to the Arrest.* The amount of space devoted by all four evangelists to the account of the Passion of Jesus is strong testimony to its paramount importance. The previous outline of events and teaching gains its significance only in the light of the climax. If Jesus was an enigma to the religious leaders and to the common people of His day, it was because He had come to fulfill a unique mission which found its fulfillment in an act of crucifixion. The sense of coming doom is unmistakable in the progressive stages of the story.

At various times previously the intentions of the leaders to kill Jesus have been mentioned, but a definite plan is decided on with the treacherous cooperation of Judas (Matt. 26:1 ff.; Mark 14:1 ff.; Luke 22:1 ff.). This betrayal from within the Twelve was already arranged before the last meeting of Jesus with the Twelve.

Even the details of the closing events have an air of destiny about them (Matt. 26:17 ff.; Mark 14:12 ff.; Luke 22:7 ff.). Someone with an upper room offers its use to Jesus for the purpose of the feast. It was arranged for a man with a pitcher to guide the disciples to it, where the meal could be prepared.

Before sitting down to the meal, Jesus washed His disciples' feet as an example in humility (John 13:1 ff.). Peter's objection that the Master should not perform for him so humble a task is overruled. As Jesus performed this service, His mind was centered on the tragedy of the betrayer, for almost immediately after resuming His seat He quoted Scripture alluding to the coming betrayal (13:18). With deep disturbance of spirit He announced that the betrayer was in the room with them. Jesus shows His feelings by offering to Judas the portion of honor. At length Judas withdrew, but it is not certain at what stage in the proceedings this happened, except that it happened before the farewell discourses.

The institution of the Lord's Supper is described in all the synoptic gospels, but not in John. Its purpose was to provide a memorial feast to draw attention to the main mission of Jesus, i.e., to shed His blood for the remission of sins. In this way He was ensuring that the memory of His work should not cease, but more than that, He was providing an interpretation of it which was to become central in the Christian church. Bread symbolized His broken body, and wine His poured-out blood, but none but He knew the significance of the feast that night. His was a lonely path to Calvary, in spite of the fact that Peter had offered to lay down his life for Him (13:37). Peter was reminded that he would deny Jesus three times before cockcrow next morning (Matt. 26:30 ff.; Mark 14:26 ff.; Luke 22:34; John 13:36 ff.).

It is not possible in an outline of this nature to detail the contents of the farewell discourses. Part (John 14) took place in the upper room, but the following parts (chs. 15, 16) form an essential unity with it. The most characteristic feature throughout is the atmosphere of calm assurance which the words of Jesus convey. There is no sense of distress on His part. Instead, He talks of His joy and peace, which the disciples will later share. There is a confidence in the perfect planning of the Father which would make anxiety incongruous. A main feature is the repeated promises regarding the Holy Spirit, who would continue the work of Jesus after He had departed.

It was possibly immediately after leaving the upper room that Jesus gave the allegory of the vine and the branches to show how important it was for the disciples to abide in Him. Their future life was to be inextricably bound up with Him. Apart from this inseparable connection, they would not be able to accomplish anything. Throughout the discourses there is much that was calculated to encourage the disciples, especially when they were to pass through tribulation. It is characteristic of the whole approach of Jesus that He shows greater concern about the disciples than about Himself in the hour of His crisis.

John records a prayer of Jesus for Himself, for the disciples, and for believers generally (ch. 17). It is deep in its revelation of the mind of Jesus. It reveals Him in close fellowship with the Father only a few hours before the cry of desolation from the cross. In that part of the prayer which concerns Himself, He prays for the Father's glory to be seen. Most of His prayer is a supplication for others – above all that they might possess the same kind of unity as He possessed with the Father.

When Gethsemane was reached, Jesus was troubled (Matt. 26:36 ff. and parallels). Was there no other way? Yet, the Father knew best. Although Jesus passed through agony in doing the Father's will, He accepted it uncomplainingly. While the bitter inner struggle went on, the three disciples specially chosen to share His sorrow fell asleep, while another was leading a band of soldiers and officers to arrest Him. It was greater sadness for Jesus to see the indifference of the three than to receive a kiss from the betrayer. Peter at least had protested His loyalty.

The arrest of Jesus set Him in noble contrast to His captors (Matt. 26:47 ff.; Mark 14:43 ff.; Luke 22:47 ff.; John 18:1 ff.). John says that some of them fell back in amazement. Peter cut off the ear of the high priest's servant. Jesus rebuked Peter and chided the multitude for bringing their swords and clubs. He offered no resistance. This was the Father's will; His hour had come, but all the disciples fled.

b. *The Passion.* There were several stages in the process which took Jesus to the cross. He was first examined in the high priest Annas' house, during which time Peter denied Him three times before cockcrow (John 18:12 ff.). It was therefore early morning. No specific charge was brought at this stage, but mockery was heaped upon Him.

It was later that Jesus was brought before the Sanhedrin (Matt. 26:57 ff. and parallels), but previously there had been much activity on the part of the officials to find false witnesses to testify against Him. It was finally agreed to proceed on the charge of threatened destruction of the Temple, linked with the charge of blasphemy. Throughout this trial the dignity of Jesus remained unimpaired in face of degrading mockery, which would have been a disgrace at any trial.

Next, Jesus was sent to Pilate because the Sanhedrin had no power to execute its own decision to have Him put to death without the governor's consent. (At this stage in Matthew's account the remorse and death of Judas is narrated to form a tragic background to the callous attitude of the religious leaders [Matt. 27:3-10]). Pilate's examination convinced him that Jesus was innocent of the charges brought against Him. In view of this, Pilate tried to avoid having to make a decision by sending Him to Herod when he learned that Jesus was a Galilean.

Herod could do nothing but mock Jesus, and Pilate was again faced with the necessity of deciding on some course of action. He decided to offer the multitude a choice between Jesus and Barabbas as the one to be released according to custom at the feast, but the multitude cried for Barabbas. In spite of a warning from his wife and his own conviction of the innocence of Jesus, Pilate at length capitulated. No more sorry figure than this Roman governor has ever disgraced the name of justice. Yet, Jesus had known beforehand that He had come to Jerusalem to be scourged and crucified.

After the governor's decision to hand Jesus over to be crucified, further mockery took place with the arraying of Jesus by the soldiers in a scarlet robe and a crown of thorns (Matt. 27:27 ff.; Mark 15:16 ff.).

Two noteworthy events occurred on the route to Calvary, where Jesus was crucified. Simon from Cyrene was forced to carry His cross (Luke 23:26 ff.) and a group of women lamented over Jesus (23:27 ff.). All the evangelists describe in detail the various stages of the crucifixion, the most cruel form of death, but none includes all the data (Matt. 27:33-56; Mark 15:33-47; Luke 23:33-49; John 19:17-37). The focal points are the dispute of Pilate with the Jews about the superscription on the cross, the reaction of the two political insurrectionists who were crucified with Jesus, the attitude of the soldiers, the jibes of the passers-by and of the chief priests and scribes, the physical signs accompanying the crucifixion, including the unnatural darkness, the sudden rending of the veil, but most of all the seven sayings of Jesus from the cross. Apart from the momentary cry of dereliction, the suffering Jesus dies triumphantly, His work fully accomplished.

The mass of detail which the evangelists have preserved about the crucifixion reflects the great importance of the event in the minds of the early Christians. There was no attempt to gloss over the shame of it. The glory of the cross was real beyond the appalling physical sufferings which the Messiah endured. The actuality of the sufferings was indispensable to the glory. When Jesus said, "It is finished," He was not thinking of His mortal life, but of His mission of redemption.

When the body of Jesus was removed from the cross, it was placed in a rich man's tomb (Matt. 27:57 ff.; Mark 15:42 ff.; Luke 23:50 ff.; John 19:38 ff.). Joseph of Arimathaea was bold enough to make special application to the governor. Matthew relates the request of the chief priests and Pharisees for the sealing of the tomb and the appointment of a guard to insure that the body was not stolen. That the fact of the burial had some importance for the early Christians is seen from a special mention of it (I Cor. 15:4).

c. *The Resurrection.* The gospels relate the fact of the resurrection of Jesus on the third day. That the tomb was empty is established by all the witnesses. There were a number of appearances of Jesus during the period between the resurrection and the ascension.

The appearances may be given as follows: (1) the appearance to Mary Magdalene (John 20:11-18); (2) to the other women (Matt. 28:9, 10); (3) to Peter (Luke 24:33-35; I Cor. 15:5); (4) to two people on the way to Emmaus (Luke 24:13-32); (5) to the ten apostles and others (Luke 24:36-43; John 20:19-25). All these occurred on one day, i.e., Easter Sunday.

The other five occurred on different days: (6) to the eleven (John 20:26-31; I Cor. 15:5); (7) to seven disciples in Galilee (John 21:1-25); (8) to the apostles and over five hundred disciples in Galilee (Matt. 28:16-20; I Cor. 15:6); (9) to James, the Lord's brother (I Cor. 15:7); (10) the concluding appearance to the apostles (Luke 24:44-53; Acts 1:1-12). In the book of Acts, Luke states in his introduction that Jesus presented Himself alive to His apostles "after his passion by many proofs, appearing to them during forty days, and speaking of the kingdom of God" (Acts 1:3). These appearances therefore were regarded by the early church as sufficient proofs of the reality of the resurrection.

Several observations are necessary concerning the character of the evidence. Beginning with Paul's list (I Cor. 15) which is clearly selective, it is not at once evident on what principle the selection has been made. It has been suggested, not improbably, that Paul's list is confined to those whose evidence had been used in preaching. This may account for the omission of specific reference to women witnesses or to the two on the Emmaus road. Whatever the reason for the selection, the evidence is invaluable, for Paul's testimony is in all probability prior to the writing of the gospels. The evidence which he cites is based on traditions which he had received.

The remaining evidence is spread throughout the gospels, although that from Mark is somewhat uncertain due to doubts about the original ending of the gospel. Nevertheless the existing ending (Mark 16:9-20) can certainly lay claim to antiquity and may well preserve an authentic tradition distinct from the rest of Mark. It appears to support the evidence for four of the appearances mentioned above (nos. 1, 4, 8, 10) all of which also occur in either Luke or John. The difficulty of unraveling the sequence of the appearances is in itself a testimony to the authenticity of the various streams of tradition. There was no collusion between the evangelists to insure an account without difficulties, nor was there the use of a common source.

One of the major problems is the difference in location of the various appearances. Those of Mark and Matthew are set in Galilee, those of Luke in Jerusalem, and those of John in Jerusalem and Galilee. Paul gives no hint of location, which suggests that in the early tradition it was not regarded as important. It should be noted that Luke shows a special interest in Jerusalem in his gospel, which may account for his exclusive selection of Jerusalem-based appearances. Those who see two conflicting traditions are driven to choose one and reject the other. There is no insuperable obstacle to both being correct, as is suggested by John's account. The journey to Galilee and back would naturally take time, but is not impossible. It is undeniable that the fact of the resurrection of Jesus is one of the best attested facts of history.

A change of attitude toward the resurrection has occurred in the realm of criticism. Earlier critics attempted to explain away the fact of the resurrection on the basis of a swoon theory, a vision theory, or a hallucination theory, but these attempts failed to square with the evidence. Now the resurrection is not explained away, but is re-interpreted, as it has been in the Bultmannian position. According to this view, the fact of the resurrection ceases to have relevance because its crucial importance is as a factor in faith rather than history. Such an emphasis tends to nullify the objective reality of the resurrection and makes it difficult to see how any common experience could be shared in the faith of all believers. The New Testament witnesses are not only varied in type, but also in the number who experienced the visitations at the same time.

Accepting therefore the fact of the resurrection as an historical event, it is next necessary to inquire what details the narratives supply about the risen Lord. (a) He was in a human form and yet His resurrection body possessed properties beyond those of normal bodies. He could pass into rooms without visible entry and could appear and disappear at will. (b) He had features which were not readily identifiable with the Jesus they had known. More than one of the stories of the appearances refer to the fact that He was not recognized. The nail prints and the familiar voice were the marks of identification. (c) There was a definite continuity with the historical Jesus, as when He conversed with and challenged Peter in a threefold way (John 21). (d) The realization of the risen Lord on the part of the disciples was the occasion of remarkable joy and transformation. That Jesus was not dead but risen changed the despair of the disciples into incredible hope. (e) The resurrection appearances were occasions for specific instruction. Acts 1:3 mentions the Kingdom and Luke 24:44 f. refers to the Scriptures and relates His present to His past teaching. It is reasonable to suppose that Jesus explained the significance of His own death and resurrection during these appearances.

The major significance of the resurrection for Christian faith was left to the early Christians to think through under the guidance of the Holy Spirit. Two factors may be mentioned. It became the first fruits for the believer's own experience. As Christ was raised from the dead, so shall the believer be. The resurrection is, therefore, the surety for the ultimate triumph of faith over the grave. Secondly, it is by the resurrection that the divine approval is shown for the work of Christ upon the cross. The resurrection is the coping stone of the whole ministry of Jesus.

d. *The Ascension.* It is only Luke among the evangelists who records this event. It took place at Bethany when, after lifting up His hands to bless the disciples, Jesus vanished from sight

(Luke 24:50, 51). Acts 1:1-11 fills in the picture with more details, the most noteworthy of which are the discussion between Jesus and the disciples regarding the restoration of the kingdom to Israel – an evidence of the disciples' current immature understanding – and the announcement of His future return by two men in white.

The disciples were not left with mere memories, but with a deep conviction that the same Lord who had companied with them in a historical sense had returned to His former glory, exalted by God and ever living to perform a high priestly function on their behalf (cf. Acts 2:36; Phil. 2:9 f.; Heb. *passim*).

8

The Teaching of Jesus

SO LARGE A proportion of the gospels is taken up with the teaching of Jesus that the importance of what He said is at once seen to be as great as what He did. He was regarded by many as a rabbi and was pleased to accept this title for Himself. Yet, the question immediately arises to what extent His teaching in methods and content can be considered typical of Jewish teachers of the first century. The populace at least were discerning enough to note one important distinction. Contrasted with the scribes, Jesus taught with authority. He did not, as they continually did, appeal to older Jewish authority. Even when He cited the Law, He claimed authority to go beyond it. Approaching His teaching, therefore, one is conscious of His uniqueness as well as His indebtedness to contemporary thought. These two aspects will be brought out in the following survey of His teaching.

A. His Teaching Methods

It will be valuable to note the major characteristics of the teaching methods of Jesus as a prelude to the study of the content, because this will help to place the teaching in its life-situation (*Sitz im Leben*).

1. *Its Adaptability*

In the gospels the first feature which strikes the reader is the way in which Jesus adapted His teaching to the type of hearer with whom He was dealing. There are many kinds of audiences mentioned. The common people gathered in crowds to hear Him and to them He spoke in parables, drawing from a wide range of everyday illustrations. He did not generally address discourses to multitudes, although a notable exception is the Sermon on the Mount, if this is to be regarded as a continuous discourse. There is a marked difference in the style of His teaching to the Galilean crowds and to the intelligentsia in Jerusalem. Further, the synoptic gospels draw a distinction between His teaching to the multitudes and His teaching to the Twelve, for the latter portion of the ministry of Jesus is devoted to the disciples.

There is no doubt that for Jesus the teaching ministry was a means to an end. As far as the Twelve were concerned, it was part of the process of training, although without question Jesus also had in mind the future ministry of the church and the incomparable value that His teaching was then to have. This factor of adaptability is particularly seen in His readiness to use every opportunity to impart some spiritual truth, whether it was an ordinary incident such as a rich young ruler's request to Him, or some festival occasion as the Feast of Tabernacles. It is not surprising that the high priests' officers sent to arrest Jesus returned without Him, but with a deep impression of His incomparable teaching. A further illustration of His adaptability was the readiness of Jesus to impart teaching to an audience of one if occasion demanded.

2. *Use of Rhetoric*

Jesus is never portrayed in the role of an orator, although He used certain rhetorical devices (but always in a natural way). This may be illustrated with examples. He used the dialogue method, sometimes posing questions Himself and sometimes responding to the questions of others. The collection of controversies recorded as taking place in the Temple area, prior to the Passion, is a marked illustration. The attempts of Pharisees and Sadducees to trick Him with difficult questions were simply regarded by Him as opportunities to express principles, a process which invariably silenced His questioners. When Jesus was asked about His own authority, He posed a counter-question about the authority of John the Baptist and put His questioners on the horns of a dilemma, which effectively made them withdraw their question. In John's gospel are preserved, moreover, instances of Jesus engaging in extended dialogue with various Jewish groups (e.g., John 6), in which cases He not infrequently used rabbinical methods of argument, which would have been appreciated by His contemporaries, although the force of it may not always be apparent in modern times. An example from the synoptic gospels is the statement regarding the resurrection (Matt. 22:32). It must be recognized that even when Jesus used rabbinical methods, He was doing so to express a deeper spiritual truth than appears on the surface. The truth does not depend on the form in which it is expressed, but on the validity which it possesses.

3. *Logical Devices*

On occasions Jesus used various logical devices which are worth noting. An example of *a fortiori* type of argument may be seen in the Sermon on the Mount, where Jesus proceeds from the lesser example of the heavenly Father's care for the birds to the greater example of His care for men. "Are you not of more value than they?" (Matt. 6:26) He asks.

Another method is *reductio ad absurdum*, a classic example of which is the controversy with the Pharisees over Beelzebub. Their charge that Jesus was casting out devils by the prince of the devils would make the devil war against himself, which is unthinkable.

The type of argument known as *ad hominem* (on the basis of an opponent's premises) was often used when Jesus appealed to the teaching of the Law. A typical example is when He cited the Law as saying, "you are gods" (John 10:34), in support of His own claim to be the Son of God.

Many times Jesus left His hearers to apply His illustrations on the strength of an analogy between the physical and spiritual worlds. Thus to demonstrate the Father's willingness to give, He appeals to what might be expected from earthly fathers (Matt. 7:9).

4. *The Use of Repetition*

One important aspect of the teaching method of Jesus was His practice of repeating His sayings. Many source theories have been based on the assumption that this did not happen, and consequently similar sayings were regarded as variant duplicates in the tradition. This method of dealing with the teaching of Jesus is open to criticism on the ground that it does not sufficiently take account of the usual practice of repetition among Jewish teachers (see B. Gerhardsson's *Memory and Manuscript* [1961], which cites evidence for this prevalent procedure). Moreover, this is a basic educational method. It cannot be expected that profound truths will be grasped at one hearing and it must be accepted that this principle was recognized by Jesus. This may well account for a considerable amount of the variation in the synoptic gospels when they report the sayings of Jesus.

Examples of repetition may be found both in content and in verbal form. Some themes, for instance, the Kingdom or the Law, frequently recur. The repetition is always purposive. In the Sermon on the Mount, there is a sequence of instances introduced by the formula, "You have heard it said . . . but I say," which heightens the effect of the distinctive teaching given. There were other techniques which Jesus used to aid the memory of His hearers. Of special interest is similarity of form, as, for instance, the Beatitudes, which would be easier to retain in the mind than a collection of dissimilar sayings.

5. *Illustrations*

No one can read the gospels without being impressed by the colorful character of Jesus' teaching. He made frequent use of metaphors, often of the most striking kind. His self-description as Light, Door, Vine, Shepherd, are drawn from common illustrations which were all the more effective because of their simplicity. He promised that His disciples would be "fishers of men" and "the salt of the earth." The contemporary Jewish teachers were "a brood of vipers." Other examples abound in the gospels. It is sufficient, however, to note that the teaching of Jesus was never dull. It was intended to be recalled. Similarly, He made constant use of similes, of which the best examples are in the parables, but by no means exclusively so. For instance, the disciples are as "sheep in the midst of wolves" (Matt. 10:16), while the Twelve are to be "wise as serpents and innocent as doves."

There can be no doubt that as a teacher Jesus possessed a sense of humor, as is seen by the extraordinary exaggerations which He sometimes mentioned. The log in the eye (Matt. 7:3 ff.) was intended to heighten the contrast with the speck, but would be wholly inappropriate as a possible obstruction in the eye. Similarly, a camel in a needle's eye (Mark 10:25) was surely not to be taken literally. With the same purpose of arresting attention is the use of paradoxical sayings, e.g., those who would be great must become slaves (Matt. 20:27), or of apparently contradictory sayings, which speak of the purpose of Jesus to divide households (Luke 12:51 ff.), although He came to bring peace.

6. *Poetic Forms*

Some of the sayings of Jesus were expressed in poetic form, no doubt to help the hearer in retaining them. C. F. Burney, in his book *The Poetry of our Lord* (1925), has given detailed attention to the formal elements of Hebrew poetry in the discourses of Jesus. He draws special attention to the methods of parallelism, rhythm and rhyme, which were characteristic of Hebrew poetry, and he is convinced that the teaching of Jesus could provide many instances of these characteristics. Only a few examples will be given to illustrate the poetic skill of Jesus. Parallelism had three main forms, synonymous, antithetic, and synthetic. In the first, a statement is made in two successive lines, the second of which repeats the first in different words. Take, for example, Mark 4:30, where Jesus asks, "With what can we compare the Kingdom of God, or what parable shall we use for it?" This method effectively emphasizes the thought. The second type, antithesis, is a statement in which the second line denies the opposite of the first, or merely states the opposite of the first by way of contrast. Matthew 20:16 serves as an example, "So the last shall be first and the first last" (cf. also Mark 4:25 and John 3:6). Throughout the teaching of Jesus antithesis was powerfully used, especially in John's gospel, not only in the themes used, such as light and darkness, truth and falseness, "my disciples" and "the world," but also in the actual forms of the sayings, for instance John 5:29, where doers of good are contrasted with doers of evil; John 11:9, 10 – walking in the day contrasted with walking in the night; and John 15:2 – bearing fruit with not bearing fruit. Synthetic parallelism is where the second line enlarges upon the thought of the first. There is a sequence of such sayings in Mathew 23:5-10, of which the first only need be cited, "They make their phylacteries broad and their fringes long." Sufficient has been said to show that Jesus made use of the usual devices of Hebrew poetry to make His teaching more easy to assimilate.

Some comment needs to be made on the subject of rhythm and rhyme, since these elements, if found in the sayings of Jesus, would focus even greater attention on the artistic methods which

He employed. The form of the statement, "Do not give dogs what is holy; and do not throw your pearls before swine" (Matt. 7:6), has an unmistakable rhythmic quality, which could be illustrated in many other sayings. This demonstrates again that Jesus was not unmindful of the form of His teaching. It is not possible to illustrate Burney's claim that Jesus used rhyme. Burney has first to translate the sayings of Jesus into Galilean Aramaic to demonstrate his contention, and not all scholars would follow his reconstructions. It is important, however, to recognize the Aramaic medium used by Jesus and to consider the possibility that He used every literary device to make His teaching more effective.

7. *The Influence of the Old Testament*

The teaching of Jesus was without doubt influenced by the Old Testament. He was constantly making use of allusions to Old Testament incidents in such a way as to appeal to the knowledge of the hearers. The reference to Lot's wife, for instance, is not enlarged upon, but knowledge of the details of the story is assumed (Luke 17:29). Similarly, the allusions to Solomon's magnificence (Matt. 6:29) or to the queen of the south's persistence (Matt. 12:42) are remarkably concise and incidental. This emphasizes an important feature about the teaching of Jesus. It was addressed to people who were versed in Old Testament ideas and who were able to understand the allusions. Any attempt, therefore, to interpret the teaching of Jesus apart from its Old Testament background would be to wrench it out of its proper context.

This factor is further borne out by the gospels, which show that Jesus' work of teaching was a direct continuation of the preaching of John the Baptist, who is portrayed in terms which suggest that he is the last of the Old Testament type prophets. It is not without significance that Jesus began proclaiming the same message as John about the need for repentance owing to the imminence of the Kingdom (cf. Mark 1:4, 14). At the same time, the teaching of Jesus soon went beyond that of John, whose task was essentially preparatory.

8. *Parabolic Forms*

The most characteristic form in the teaching of Jesus is the parable, which was particularly used in the latter part of His ministry. The purpose of the parabolic form has often been debated, especially in view of the statement of Jesus that this form was used "because seeing they do not see, and hearing they do not hear, nor do they understand" (Matt. 13:13; cf. Mark 4:11, 12; Luke 8:9, 10). It is certain that Jesus did not use this form to obscure the message, and His words must exclude such a meaning. There is no doubt that a parable is relatively easy to remember and for that reason caused people to think. Those spurred on by no more than idle curiosity would gain nothing, and in this sense would be unable to see or understand.

Many problems have surrounded the interpretation of the parables, which cannot be discussed here. It must be noted, however, that it is this form of the teaching of Jesus which has led to many misunderstandings. Some schools of interpretation have considered that spiritual importance must attach to every detail of the story (e.g., the allegorical school). Others have gone to the opposite extreme and restricted the point of the parable to one generally applicable principle of a moral kind (moralizing school). Others have considered the eschatological relevance to be uppermost (eschatological school). No interpretation which does not relate the parable to the historic situation of Jesus is likely to be correct. Joachim Jeremias (*The Parables of Jesus* [Eng. tr. by S. H. Hooke, 1962]) has done this, but he excises many supposed influences which he considers to have obscured their original form. The interpreter may make good sense of the life situation of these parables without resorting to editorial methods.

One or two of the parables recorded are more in the nature of allegories, e.g., the Sower and the Tares. These come nearest to the allegorical forms found in the fourth gospel (Shepherd and Vine allegories). There are also many sayings in John which are parabolic in style although not in form; but too rigid a distinction must not be drawn between the synoptic gospels and the Johannine tradition in this field (cf. C. H. Dodd, *Historical Tradition in the Fourth Gospel* [1963]).

B. The Content of the Teaching of Jesus

When an attempt is made to produce a summary of the teaching of Jesus, the difficulties of classifying it in a concise manner are at once apparent, for different scholars select different aspects as being of most importance. Nevertheless, a useful summary may be produced, provided it is borne in mind throughout that Jesus was not a dogmatic theologian. What He taught had an essentially practical value, and it is necessary to examine the teaching as a whole to obtain a satisfactory concept of it. Some effort has therefore been made to classify the teaching under major themes.

1. *Teaching About God*

There are three main aspects in the teaching of Jesus about God – as Creator, Father, and King. It will be noted that these aspects are expressed in terms of activities rather than as attributes, but the latter are not excluded. The creatorship of God is seen especially in teaching on His providential care for His creatures. That God was Creator of the world is assumed rather than explicitly stated. The clearest statement is in Mark 13:19 – "the creation which God created." That Jesus taught a special providential care is seen particularly in His statements regarding the heavenly Father's care for and knowledge of such creatures as sparrows (Matt. 10:31). It was basic to the teaching of Jesus that God watched over the whole creation.

It is in the realm of God's fatherhood that the uniqueness of Jesus' teaching becomes most evident. Israel had learned to conceive of God as Father, because Israel as a corporate whole was viewed as God's son. Sonship in this sense, however, was national rather than individual. It was not until Jesus taught it that men considered the possibility of a personal relationship with God. Certainly His Jewish contemporaries, with their transcendental view of God, could not conceive that He could be thought of in terms of intimate fellowship. As a mode of address in Jewish prayers, "Our Father" is not unknown (cf. G. F. Moore, *Judaism* [1927-30], II, 202 ff.). The use by Jesus of such expressions as "Your heavenly Father knows," however, or the whole approach to God seen in the Lord's Prayer strike a new note. Men accustomed to approach God with holy fear would find incredible the insistence on the father-son relationship in the teaching of Jesus. This was the unique feature in His approach. It should be remembered that the idea of men being sons of God has as its basis the fact that God is the Father of Jesus. At the same time Jesus drew a distinction between man's sonship and His own sonship. The most striking illustration of this distinction is found in John 20:17, when Jesus said to Mary that she was to report to the disciples, "I am ascending to my Father and your Father, to my God and to your God." Man's sonship cannot, of course, be considered apart from the divine Son, but the distinction must be maintained.

At the baptism of Jesus a heavenly voice attested His divine sonship, and this may be regarded as normative for His whole ministry. He was not called as the prophets were to a specific task, but was attested as possessing a specific status. It was in the consciousness of this status that He executed His ministry in obedience to the Father's will. Nowhere is this brought out more forcefully than in John's gospel, where Father and Son are seen in such close relationship. It is on the strength of His consciousness of His own special relationship with God that Jesus brings to men the concept of God as their own Father. Even though they had had the word on their lips previous to His teaching, they had never entered into the spirit of it. God had never before become such a living reality as the heavenly Father. This was no mere accepted formula, but adoption into a new family relationship.

It was maintained by T. W. Manson (*The Teachings of Jesus* [1945], 113 ff.) that the Lord's Prayer contains a concise summary of the main aspects of Jesus' teaching on the Fatherhood of God. He sees two main divisions, the Father as sovereign arbiter of world history and the Father who cares for and ministers to each child.

Under the first division the focus is upon God as a person to be glorified (cf. Matt. 5:16). The prayer for the coming of the Kingdom is in accordance with the Father's pleasure (Luke 12:32). It is the Father's appointment that men should possess a kingdom (Luke 22:29). The necessity for God's will to be done is an integral part of Jesus' own relation to the Father, as is seen in the prayer in Gethsemane (Mark 14:36).

Under the second main division there are three requests in the Lord's Prayer which draw attention to different facets of the Father's care for His children. Daily bread is indispensable, and Jesus therefore assured His disciples, "Your Father knows that you have need of these things" (i.e., food and clothing) (Matt. 6:32; Luke 12:30). Next, forgiveness of sins is requested, and again the request may be echoed from the sayings of Jesus elsewhere (cf. Matt. 6:14 f.; Mark 11:25). The third request is for protection and deliverance, and this draws further attention to that providential care which was noted under the creatorship of God.

No one can consider these aspects of the teaching of Jesus about God without being impressed by the closeness of the relationship between Him and the Father and between the Father and His earthly children. Whatever parallels in terminology may be found in the rabbinical writings, there is nothing in them to compare with the sense of filial obedience and affection toward God inculcated by Jesus, of which He Himself was the best example.

The third aspect of God – as King – will be more fully dealt with under the heading of the Kingdom. But no true approach can be made to the Kingdom without recognizing that its basis is the character of God as King. This involves not only the concept of majesty, but also of sovereignty. It is assumed that what God has purposed He is competent to bring to fruition. It is, therefore, taken for granted throughout that His designs cannot ultimately be thwarted. The teaching of Jesus regarding the Kingdom, which will be considered in the next section, is supported by the absolute certainty of the final triumph of God in His world.

2. *Teaching About the Kingdom*

a. *Various schools of thought.* Undoubtedly the Kingdom teaching of Jesus must be ranked among the most important themes. Much debate has been occasioned by it, and it will, therefore, be necessary to give a careful definition of the concept to avoid confusion. The notion of a Kingdom in the sense of a community over which a king reigns is not the dominant concept. It is, rather, the rule of God which is uppermost. This, however, needs further definition in the light of the various uses of the term by Jesus. These uses may conveniently be grouped under two categories: (a) those announcing a future Kingdom and (b) those announcing a present Kingdom. The existence of these two aspects has created a real problem in interpretation. Many have considered them to be mutually exclusive and have, therefore, rejected one or the other of them.

The view that for Jesus the concept of the Kingdom was wholly eschatological was strongly maintained by Johannes Weiss (*Die Predigt Jesu vom Reiche Gottes* [2nd. ed. 1900]) and Albert

Schweitzer (*op. cit.*), whose interpretation has come to be known as Consistent Eschatology. According to this view, the apocalyptic elements in the teaching of Jesus are the most important elements, and His mission is to be understood as wholly eschatological. Moreover, it is said that Jesus expected this eschatological event to take place in His lifetime. There have been many modifications of this eschatological view since Schweitzer's interpretation, but there is still support for the basic presuppositions behind it. Thus for Rudolf Bultmann, Jesus is seen as an apocalyptic prophet who expected the imminent arrival of the Kingdom (*Theology of the New Testament*, I [Eng. tr. 1952], 22). A similar position is adopted by M. Werner, *Formation of Christian Dogma* (1957), 9-27 and R. H. Fuller, *The Mission and Achievement of Jesus* (1954), 25 ff., who both maintain that Jesus' teaching on the Kingdom was eschatological.

A strong movement in reaction to this school of thought may be termed the non-eschatological interpretation of the Kingdom. This was the view taken by T. W. Manson (*op. cit.*), who regarded the Kingdom as coming in the experience of individuals. The Kingdom is not eschatological, but present. It is God's will being done here and now, supremely in the obedience of Jesus. The mission of Jesus was to lead others into a similar experience, and the mission of the church is to win the world for Christ. Since, when this is done, there will be no need for an eschatological consummation, the eschatological interpretation can be dispensed with.

Many others have taken up a similar view, such as F. C. Grant (*The Gospel of the Kingdom* [1946]) and J. W. Bowman (*Prophetic Realism and the Gospel* [1955]). The former of these considers that Jesus' Kingdom teaching was a social gospel, while the latter propounds a theory of prophetic realism which conceives of the Kingdom in terms of present personal relationships between God and man. But it is C. H. Dodd who has suggested the most thorough-going non-eschatological view by his theory of realized eschatology, by which he means that Jesus' original teaching was that the Kingdom had already arrived (cf. *The Apostolic Preaching and its Developments*, [2nd ed. 1944]). He finds his support for his theory in Paul's eschatology and in that of the fourth gospel. The apocalyptic language of Jesus is regarded as symbolic. Another advocate of non-eschatological Kingdom teaching was William Manson (*Jesus the*

Messiah, 1946), who confined the Kingdom to an inner consciousness in men.

Since both of these opposing views were obliged to explain away the alternative elements, they were equally unsatisfactory, and it is not surprising that various attempts have been made to find a synthesis between the present and future aspects of the Kingdom. Such a synthesis has gained considerable support and would seem to be the most reasonable deduction from the evidence. The difference between different interpreters is due to different ideas of how the Kingdom is a present reality. Some maintain that the Kingdom is present only in the person and acts of Jesus; others, that it is timeless and can therefore be present and future at the same time; still others, that the Kingdom is essentially the powerful activity of God and is immediate, although the fullest consummation is future; still others, that the Kingdom is essentially future, but is so near that its effects have spilled over into the present; and yet others, that the Kingdom must be understood existentially, in which case time ceases to have relevance for it. It is impossible here to discuss these various views, but enough has been said to demonstrate the complexity of understanding precisely what Jesus meant when He spoke of the Kingdom. At the same time, we shall not be amiss if we recognize that the teaching of Jesus cannot be understood unless room is made for both present and future aspects. Some attempt will now be made to summarize the main facets of this Kingdom teaching.

b. *The Kingdom as Present.* The more important sayings which set forth the present reality of the Kingdom will first be enumerated. Luke 17:20, 21 records the saying, "the Kingdom of God is in the midst of you (*entos*)," which might alternatively be rendered "within you." This appears to demand some present realization, whichever interpretation is followed. Another saying is one found in both Matthew 12:28 and Luke 11:20, where Jesus refers to the exorcism of demons and adds, "If it is by the Spirit of God that I cast out demons, then the Kingdom of God has come upon you." Here the present reality of the Kingdom is again unmistakable. The nature of the present realization is seen as a triumph over evil agencies. When Jesus referred to the violent entering the Kingdom (Matt. 11:11 f.; Luke 7:28), He was relating His statement to John the Baptist, and the words seem to mean that those who are now in the Kingdom are greater than John, because he was before the Kingdom. The enigmatic reference to men of violence taking the Kingdom by force also draws attention to a present activity. Much discussion has surrounded the meaning of this verse. Some take the verb passively as meaning "to suffer violence," while others regard it as middle voice and as meaning "to act violently." The latter of these renderings is more probably correct and gives a more dynamic force to the statement. It is worth noting that violence was being directed against John the Baptist, whom Jesus identified as the hoped-for Elijah. A fourth important passage testifying to the present reality of the Kingdom is Matthew 21:31 (cf. Luke 11:52), where Jesus states that tax-collectors and harlots enter the Kingdom before the chief priests and scribes.

c. *Aspects of the Kingdom.* Sufficient has been said to show that Jesus Himself taught a present experience of the Kingdom. But it is necessary to outline briefly in what that experience consists. G. E. Ladd (*Jesus and the Kingdom*, 1964) has focused attention on three aspects of this, which will serve admirably as a summary of the teaching. The first is the Kingdom as dynamic power. The concept here is of a spiritual conquest over spiritual forces. The many instances of exorcism in the gospels are evidence of the dynamic power of Jesus over the spiritual adversaries. The binding of the strong man armed, in one of the parables of Jesus (Luke 11:21, 22), is symbolic of His ministry and of the present realization of the Kingdom. In this connection the remark of Jesus when the seventy returned from their mission of announcing the Kingdom is significant, "I saw Satan fall like lightning from heaven" (Luke 10:18). The whole concept of the ministry is dynamic, consisting not only in words but in healing deeds. The authority of Jesus in His teaching bears the mark of the present reality of His Kingdom and differentiates it from the hopes of the scribes.

Secondly, it is important to note that in all His teaching Jesus made it clear that the Kingdom is God's, not man's. The mission of Jesus was the mission of God in redemptive activity. Ladd brings into his considerations here the fact that God is a seeking, inviting, fatherly, and judging God. In other words, he deduces the nature of the Kingdom from the nature of God. But as it is God's Kingdom, it differs from all other kingdom concepts. It is supernatural in character.

Thirdly, the whole concept of salvation must be related to

the present character of the Kingdom. Ladd speaks here of the aspect of salvation which is present and links with this the gift which God now gives to the members of the Kingdom, i.e., salvation and righteousness. This is an attempt to integrate the salvation teaching of Jesus with the Kingdom concept. If the Kingdom is central in Jesus' teaching, then all other aspects of His teaching must be related to it.

Membership in the Kingdom is, therefore, for those who receive God's gift of salvation. This distinguishes it at once from any notions of a materialistic or nationalistic Kingdom. It makes clear, moreover, that the Kingdom will not be established by the converting of the world to the Christian faith. Jesus never foresaw a universal acceptance of the Gospel, as the parable of the Sower and the Seeds shows. It is nevertheless a Kingdom which could be the subject of prayer for its establishment, as is seen by the petition, "Thy Kingdom come," in the Lord's Prayer. The uttering of such a prayer expresses a desire for a fuller realization of what is already taking place. The constant emphasis on repentance and faith as prerequisites for approach to God demonstrates the essentially spiritual nature of the Kingdom. More will be said later about the ethics of the Kingdom.

d. *The Eschatological Event.* This aspect of the Kingdom is equally important and must be given full weight. It is undeniable that, in addition to viewing the Kingdom as present, Jesus also looked toward a future event. These two aspects are complementary. In the eschatological discourse in Matthew 24, Mark 13, and Luke 21, Jesus used apocalyptic imagery in such a way that some kind of catastrophic event in the future, in the *eschaton,* must be understood. The best way to incorporate both present and future aspects of the Kingdom is by maintaining that the same Kingdom, which at present exists in a dynamic form in the activity of God among men, will receive its consummation in an event at the end of history. These two aspects are brought into close proximity in the Kingdom parables, which must next be considered.

e. *The Parables of the Kingdom.* First, they illustrate the growth of the Kingdom. It will not be established by irresistible power, but by action akin to the growth of seed. The most evident feature here is the fact that only one of the four types of soil mentioned in the parable of the Sower is productive. There is a considerable element of mystery about the Kingdom, which is given only to some to understand. The unexpected character of the Kingdom is illustrated by the parable of the Tares, where the distinction between the true and the false was not at once apparent. Indeed, separation will not take place until the *eschaton.* The Kingdom in its present state cannot, therefore, be considered as an identifiable entity.

The same quality of unexpectedness is seen in the parable of the Mustard Seed. Smallness is difficult to reconcile with the divine Kingdom, but there is a marked contrast between its beginnings and its end state. This is the main point of the parable. The present is related to the future as the mustard seed to the tree. Jesus' contemporaries could see only the seed, but He looked beyond to the further demonstration of the Kingdom.

A similar truth is taught in the parable of the Leaven, where the imperceptibility of the operation of the Kingdom is in mind. Some problem exists over the fact that the whole lump of dough is leavened, which has sometimes been regarded as illustrating the permeation of evil within the church and sometimes of the permeation of good in the world through the church. But neither interpretation is as probable as that which sees the ultimate triumph of the Kingdom at the consummation of the existing world order.

Two parables, the Treasure and the Pearl, draw attention to the value of the Kingdom. It does not appear worthwhile to all but those who are discerning will recognize its inestimable worth exceeding all other values. On the other hand, the parable of the Net reminds the hearer that, for the time being, some who do not deserve it will share in the benefits of the Kingdom until the final establishment of it.

That the Kingdom of God is not to be restricted to Jews is clear from the parable of the Vineyard, which was addressed to the Jewish leaders and which concluded with the statement "the Kingdom of God will be taken away from you and given to a nation producing the fruits of it" (Matt. 21:43). This aspect of universality of the Kingdom is also found in Matthew 8:11, 12. In both these passages the Jews receive the offer of the Kingdom before the Gentiles. The Kingdom applies not only to all nationalities, but to all classes within nations (cf. Matt. 12:31). This latter thought comes in the application of the parable of the Two Sons, which stresses the need for repentance and faith.

The parable of the Marriage Feast in Matthew 22 shows the

fate of those who scorn or ignore the summons of the Kingdom. This once again seems to point to the rejection of the Kingdom by the Jewish people and differentiates the Kingdom of God from their nationalistic concepts.

It remains to note the relationship of the Kingdom to the Church. Many exegetes have identified the two, but this is difficult for several reasons. Nowhere does Jesus describe His disciples exclusively as members of the Kingdom. Moreover, the Church appears to have arisen out of the Kingdom. It is the Church's task to witness to the Kingdom, and the Church is the instrument and custodian of the Kingdom. Ladd maintains that they are separate concepts, one taking its point of departure from God, the other from men (*op. cit.*, 258-273).

f. *The Ethics of the Kingdom.* The problem of the ethics of Jesus is important in this context. No survey of the teaching of Jesus can in fact ignore the predominant place which ethical injunctions have in the total sayings of Jesus. Yet it is the ethical teaching which has been most paralleled in Jewish ethical sayings and instructions, and this raises the problem of the extent to which the ethics of Jesus can be considered unique. Even though many of the individual sayings of Jesus may be paralleled, the over-all impression of the Jewish ethical teaching is legalistic, whereas the teaching of Jesus breathes a different atmosphere. It is no longer conformity to law, whether written or oral, but the pursuance of the will of God understood as the norm for the Kingdom of God.

Our purpose is only to draw attention to the salient features of the ethics of Jesus in relation to the Kingdom teaching. The first characteristic is that the authority for the ethics rests in the authority of Jesus who rejected several scribal interpretations of the Law and modified the whole approach to ceremonial observances. The basis of Jesus' own authority for ethics was His claim to fulfill perfectly the will of God. Secondly, it is noted that the ethical teaching is an essential feature of both the present and future aspects of the Kingdom. Where God's rule is active, that rule must find expression in behavior which befits the character of God. This is essentially the religious sanction in Christian ethics. It is not the sole sanction, for the eschatological aspect is equally important. There is no support for excluding either, and such a one-sided view as Schweitzer's *Interimsethik* must be rejected (i.e. that the ethic of Jesus was intended only to be temporary).

What Jesus taught was of more than passing significance. It possessed eternal validity and is as relevant to the present age as to the future. This does not mean that there are no difficulties in fulfilling the ethical demands. To love one's neighbor as oneself and, even more, to love one's enemies makes absolute demands upon any man. There can be no denying that these demands are an expression of divine love.

One special facet of the ethics of Jesus is the emphasis on inner motives. Such things as anger, hatred, restraint, humility, cannot be judged by external law. They belong not to adherence to a code of rules, but to the manifestation of character (cf. Luke 6:45). The demands of Jesus are exacting – even careless words will have to be accounted for (Matt. 12:36). Moreover, the claims of the Kingdom are such that they must at times take precedence over family ties (cf. Matt. 10:34-39; Luke 9:60, 61). Indeed the ethic of Jesus involves self-denial (Matt. 16:24), which means that the claims of the Kingdom must take precedence even over the claims of self. There is no other ethical system which demands the negation of the existing order to such an extent as to require the hating of one's own life (Luke 14:26). Self ceases to matter. The affairs of the Kingdom are of paramount importance.

It is extraordinary how much is said about rewards in the teaching of Jesus (cf. Matt. 5:12, 46; 6:4, 18; 18:1-4). The idea of return for merit, which was conspicuous in the theology of the Jews, is certainly not absent from the teaching of Jesus, but His teaching goes beyond this. The parable about the laborers in the vineyard admirably illustrates this point (Matt. 20:1-10). The first group of laborers worked a whole day for a day's pay; that was merit. The last group worked only an hour for a day's pay; that was an act of grace. The basis of rewards in the ethics of Jesus is wholly different from normal human reckoning. The men of the Kingdom must be prepared for new standards.

3. *Jesus' Testimony Concerning Himself*

The evidence from the teaching of Jesus regarding His own person may be conveniently summarized under two main classifications: the names which He applied to Himself and the specific references to His person. Under the first heading it is important to distinguish those names which He applied to Himself from those applied to Him by others.

a. *The Names That Jesus Used of Himself.* The most widely used was Son of man and it will be well to begin with this, especially as in the gospels it is found only on the lips of Jesus. A considerable amount of literature has gathered around His use of the term in an endeavor to discover what He meant by it, but it will be possible here to give only a brief survey of the major considerations. The different interpreters may be classified in two groups, those who hold that Jesus Himself used the title and those who reject such a view. Clearly if the latter group is correct, the Son of man passages do not belong to the teaching of Jesus and should not be further considered for our immediate purpose. It is necessary, therefore, to comment on this point of view before proceding to outline the self-testimony of Jesus.

On what grounds are the Son of man sayings regarded either as unauthentic or else interpreted of someone other than Jesus Himself? First, to take the view that most of the sayings are unauthentic, mention may be made of P. Vielhauer, who rejects those sayings about the Son of man's earthly work and those about His sufferings, and deals only with those referring to His glory. But even these he denies to Jesus because of the lack of connection between the Kingdom of God and the Son of man sayings. His deduction is that since one of these (the Kingdom) is authentic, the other cannot be, but apart from the fact that this appears to be a *non sequitur,* the preservation of both lines of tradition in the gospels, without any apparent incongruity, militates against this view (H. E. Todt fully discusses it in his *Der Menschensohn in der synoptischen Uberlieferung* [1959], 298-316). Bultmann (*Theology of the New Testament I* [1951], 29) considered the Son of man passion sayings as *vaticinia ex eventu,* but without adequate basis. A comparison of the three passion predictions (cf. Matt. 16:21; 17:22, 23; 20:18, 19) shows that the evangelists had no doubt that Jesus intended the Son of man to be understood as Himself. It will not do to regard these sayings as community creations, for in that case the use of the title becomes doubly unintelligible.

There are many advocates for the view that Jesus used the title, but that it was the church which identified Him with the title (cf. Todt, *op. cit.* and A. J. B. Higgins, *Jesus and the Son of Man* [1964]). It is impossible for our present purpose to discuss the detailed evidence on the grounds of which it is maintained that Jesus did not use the title of Himself, but the following survey will proceed on the assumption that Jesus meant to call Himself Son of man (cf. O. Cullmann, *The Christology of the New Testament* [1959]).

It will be convenient to group the sayings according to the classification already mentioned. First to be considered are the sayings connected with the earthly work of Jesus. Mark records two such sayings, 2:10 (on the authority to forgive sins) and 2:27 (on the lordship of the Sabbath). Matthew and Luke share four such sayings (Matt. 5:11; 8:20; 11:19; 12:32; Luke 6:22; 7:34; 9:58; 12:10). Luke alone has one (19:10) and Matthew alone has two (13:37; 16:13). On the most straightforward understanding of these passages it is inescapable that Jesus intends Himself to be understood as the Son of man. Mark 2:10 and 2:27 attribute to Him special authority. It is God who is generally spoken of as forgiving sins and it is God who ordained the Sabbath. It is difficult to avoid the conclusion that Jesus was making a high claim for Himself, unless these passages are regarded as not originating in Jesus (Higgins, for instance, sees them as community products).

In the four shared by Matthew and Luke it appears equally clear that Jesus is referring to Himself. Men will hate the disciples on account of Jesus. The Son of man is contrasted with John the Baptist in such a way that the title must be understood of Jesus Himself. Moreover, the Son of man has nowhere to lay His head, which fact relates to Jesus' own itinerant ministry. And while blasphemy against the Holy Spirit cannot be forgiven, blasphemy against the Son of man can be. All of these instances are intelligible if Jesus is describing Himself, although it still needs to be examined why He chose to use this title rather than the simple "I." A comparison of Matthew 16:13 with Mark 8:27 shows how both forms have been preserved for the same question. Matthew has, "Who do men say that the Son of man is?", whereas Mark has, "Who do men say that I am?" Since in both narratives Peter confesses Christ in the same form of words, "You are the Christ," the conclusion is inescapable that the disciples understood Jesus to mean Himself.

Of the sayings connected with the sufferings of Jesus most are in Mark and are shared by the other synoptists (cf. Mark 8:31; 9:12, 31; 10:33 f., 45; 14:21, 41; cf. also Luke 17:25; 22:48; 24:7; and Matt. 26:2). These statements show that as Jesus anticipated His passion, He made increasing use of the title. Its meaning for Him was inextricably bound up with His work of redemption.

The third group of sayings all have an eschatological emphasis and in this case there are more in Matthew than in Mark (cf. Mark 8:38; 9:9; 13:26; 14:62; Luke (with parallels in Matthew) 1:30; 12:8, 40; 17:24, 26; Luke (alone) 17:22, 30; 18:8b; 21:36; Matthew (alone) 10:23; 13:41; 16:27, 28; 19:28; 24:30, 39b; 25:31). There is clearly a strong tradition behind these sayings and some are inclined to accept an authenticity for them which they deny for the other groups. But it is difficult to maintain that Jesus reserved the title for His part in eschatological events and for no other purpose. This would have meaning only if the title had an accepted eschatological significance. But the sayings themselves gain in meaning if Jesus used the title in connection with His earthly work as well as for His future heavenly functions.

The two main aspects in the use of the title are therefore suffering and glory, and there is much to be said for the view that the title is a synthesis of the suffering servant of Isaiah and of the "son of man" in Daniel 7:13 f. This led T. W. Manson (*The Teaching of Jesus* [1931] 211 ff., *The Servant Messiah* [1953] 72-74) to regard the title as corporate, supposing that Jesus was including His disciples in the title. But it is difficult to believe that the disciples or any others would have understood it in this sense. It makes little difference what the antecedents of the title were unless they were recognized by Jesus' contemporaries. A distinction must, however, be made between what Jesus Himself meant by it and what the disciples and others understood by it. It may be regarded as an Aramaic expression meaning either man in general or man in particular. The latter seems the only reasonable proposition of the two. It may be that at least to the disciples Jesus was The Man *par excellence*. But for Himself the title no doubt carried far deeper significance. He probably chose it as the most suitable alternative to the title "Messiah," which He avoided for political reasons.

The titles Son of David, Son of God, and Messiah, although used of Him by others, were not used specifically by Jesus Himself. They do not therefore enter into the present discussion.

Yet attention must be drawn to the fact that Jesus did implicitly accept them. In the case of His Sonship, His teaching in John's gospel is full of references to His filial relationship with God. The title Son of God is therefore seen to be highly applicable to express that relationship.

b. *Other Indications.* What other evidence is there in the gospels regarding Jesus' view of Himself? There is more to assist here in John's gospel than in the other gospels. Jesus frequently speaks of Himself as being sent. He is deeply conscious of His mission to do the Father's will (e.g. John 5:17). He knows that He is sent for a specific purpose that no one else can fulfill. His testimony to Himself comes out vividly in the great "I AM" statements in this gospel. "I am the way, the truth and the life" (John 14:6) is a unique claim. The same may be said of "I am the resurrection and the life" (11:25). No less far-reaching is His claim to be the light of the world (8:12), which could hardly be more comprehensive and universal.

It is difficult to escape the conclusion that in the mind of Jesus there was a connection with the great I AM as the name of Jehovah in the Old Testament, particularly in view of the statement of John 8:58, "Before Abraham was, I am." In the synoptic gospels the saying of Jesus nearest to the Johannine evidence is found in Matthew 11:27, which is a clear claim to uniqueness of filial relationship (but see also the accounts of Jesus' baptism). Yet there are also hints in all the gospels, but especially in John, that Jesus was conscious of human limitations. He knew hunger and thirst and the need for sleep and rest. He could express anger and could show compassion. He needed prayer to sustain Him. But the human side, as we should expect, comes out more clearly in His actions than in His teaching.

4. The Teaching About the Work of Christ

The mission of Jesus was many-sided, but His special work was concerned with the significance of the passion. This forms the focal point of the gospel narratives, and all that precedes it must be interpreted in the light of it. The Kingdom teaching, for instance, is seen in its true perspective only in the light of the cross.

Before examining the statements of Jesus relating to His own work, there are some preliminary observations which must be made. There is no doubt, to begin with, that Jesus regarded

His mission as a direct fulfillment of Scripture. He stated His purpose to be fulfillment of the Law (Matt. 5:17). In the upper room, after the reference to the betrayal, Jesus added, "The Son of man goes as it is written of him" (Matt. 26:24), a clear allusion to the coming passion. After the Transfiguration, Mark records a question of Jesus, "and how is it written of the Son of man, that he should suffer many things and be treated with contempt?" (Mark 9:12). There are other references which add support to the view that Jesus was deeply aware that His own experience was the subject of prophecy (cf. Matt. 26:56; Luke 18:31; 24:25-27, 44, 45).

It has sometimes been supposed that in John's gospel a different account of the work of Jesus is found as compared with the synoptics. One such view is that it is the incarnation rather than the passion which is the basis of redemption. This is supported from John 6:53, where Jesus says, ". . . unless you eat the flesh of the Son of man and drink his blood you have no life in you" (cf. also 6:56). But if this is intended to relate to the incarnation it would need to be understood in a quasi-physical way. It is more in harmony with the general tenor of the teaching in the passage to understand it in a spiritual manner. Another view is that redemption is by illumination, and for this an appeal is made to such passages as John 8:12 ("I am the light of the world"), John 17:17 ("Sanctify them in the truth: thy word is truth"), John 14:9 ("He who has seen me has seen the Father"). It is undeniable that there has been an effective illumination of the mind as a result of the coming of Jesus, but it would rob the mission of Jesus of its primary purpose if it were restricted to an educative process. The death of Christ is plainly presented in the fourth gospel as the object of the incarnation, as an examination of the evidence will show.

a. *His Death As a Sacrificial Offering*. There is much evidence for this aspect of the passion of Christ. In addition to the statement in John 6 cited above, which makes it clear that Jesus conceived of His flesh and blood as having been given for the life of the world, the most important evidence comes from the words used in the institution of the Lord's Supper. The institution must be seen against an Old Testament background. It is described by Jesus as connected with the New Covenant, especially His blood which is shed "for many for the remission of sins" (Matt. 26:26-28). There can be no doubt that Jesus intended His disciples to understand that His death would result in remission of sins. The connection of this with the sacrificial system of the old Covenant seems impossible to deny. Some have treated this evidence with reserve, because the words "for the remission of sins" occur only in Matthew, but they are so fully in harmony with the whole teaching of Jesus that they cannot reasonably be disputed on those grounds. Two of the sayings of Jesus in John's gospel emphasize the finality of His work (17:4; 19:30). The latter of these statements, coming as it does direct from the cross, shows that the death itself was viewed as an accomplishment.

b. *His Death Was Voluntary.* In the good shepherd allegory, Jesus not only states that the good shepherd gives his life for his sheep (John 10:11), but that He Himself lays down His life of His own accord (John 10:18). He maintained that Pilate had no power over Him except as it was granted from above (John 19:10, 11). He made clear that no love is greater than that which sacrifices life for the sake of friends (John 15:13). In his gospel, John seems to be particularly concerned to show this aspect of the voluntary self-giving of Jesus.

c. *His Death Was a Divine Necessity.* In the fourth gospel there is a developing sense of the inevitable character of the passion, described as "the hour." Several times John mentions that his hour is not yet, until Jesus Himself says, "Father, the hour has come" (John 17:1). This sense of divine necessity is seen in the first prediction of the passion in Matthew 16:21 ff., "From that time Jesus began to show his disciples that he *must* go to Jerusalem . . . and be killed, and on the third day be raised." Compare also the angel's reminder of Jesus' words to the women at the tomb (Luke 24:7). The same idea is found in John 3:14 – "The Son of man must be lifted up." In all the gospels the death of Christ is seen as the climax to the mission of Jesus. There is no indication that it happened by accident. It was all part of a divine plan.

d. *His Death Was Substitutionary.* When Jesus identified Himself with those who attended the baptism of John and when John hesitated at the thought of baptizing Jesus (according to Matt. 3:14), Jesus said that He requested baptism because it was fitting for Him to fulfill all righteousness. Although He needed no repentance, He became one with those who did. In Luke 22:37 Jesus appeals to Isaiah 53:12 (reckoned among the transgressors) as fulfilled in Himself, which suggests that He regarded Himself in the role of the suffering servant.

There is one statement of Jesus which suggests the idea of substitution by the use of the Greek word *anti* (in the place of). It occurs in Mark 10:45 (cf. Matt. 20:28), where Jesus says that the Son of man came to give His life a ransom for *(anti)* many. The word ransom means an equivalent exchange price, and while the imagery used cannot be pressed, the idea that the Son of man did something in the stead of others is inescapable. There are, in addition, passages where a different preposition is used, but where the context suggests substitution – for instance, in the words of institution of the Lord's Supper (Matt. 26:28, "poured out for many") *peri* is used; while in the statement by Jesus that the good shepherd lays down his life for the sheep (John 10:15), *huper* is used. Some scholars (e.g. Vincent Taylor) interpret these prepositions as expressing representation rather than substitution, but in neither case would this do full justice to the meaning.

e. *His Death Was a Triumph Over the Devil.* When the conflict of the passion became imminent and Judas had already betrayed his Master with a kiss, Jesus conceded to those who arrested Him ". . . this is your hour, and the power of darkness" (Luke 22:53). Moreover, when Jesus referred to His death in the figure of a grain of wheat falling to the ground (John 12:23), He went on to announce, "Now is the judgment of this world; now shall the ruler of this world be cast out" (John 12:31). He must have had something of this intense spiritual conflict in mind in His parable of the strong man who needed first to be bound before his goods could be seized (Matt. 12:29). In a strong denunciation of Herod, Jesus told the Pharisees to go and report to that fox, Herod, "I cast out demons and perform cures today and tomorrow, and the third day I finish my course" (Luke 13:32).

f. *His Death Is Applicable Only Through Repentance and Faith.* At the commencement of His ministry Jesus preached the imminence of the Kingdom and exhorted men to repent and believe the Gospel (Mark 1:14, 15). That Gospel involved the whole of His mission, which centered on His death. His mission was never designed for righteous people, but for sinners willing to repent (Matt. 9:12, 13; Mark 2:17; Luke 5:31, 32). There are many allusions to faith in the teaching of Jesus, and it is clear that He conceived of no other means by which the benefits of His work might be appropriated (cf. John 3:16; 5:24; 6:29). One of the immediate results for those who come to Jesus in response to His invitation and join themselves to His mission is that they find spiritual rest (Matt. 11:28). There can be no doubt that Jesus desired a radical change to be effected in the lives of those who followed Him on the basis of His mission.

5. *The Teaching About the Holy Spirit*

The synoptic gospels have considerably less teaching about the Spirit than John's gospel, but there are nevertheless some significant statements. Jesus makes clear His own consciousness of the Spirit's part in His mission. In Matthew 12:28 He says, "If it is by the Spirit of God that I cast out demons, then the kingdom of God has come upon you." It is true that in the parallel passage in Luke, "the Spirit" is replaced by "the finger of God," but there can be no doubt that this alternative must be interpreted in the light of Matthew's text. Particularly is this necessary since the statement comes within the context of the Beelzebub controversy (see below). Here then is the claim that Jesus' activity in the spiritual realm is by the Spirit of God. When at the commencement of His ministry Jesus applied the prophecy of Isaiah 61:1, 2 to Himself, it was evidence of His own specific claim to the Spirit's power. This was no doubt closely linked in the mind of Jesus with the descent of the Spirit on the occasion of His baptism and also His consciousness of being led by the Spirit to the place of temptation.

The blasphemy saying, which occurs in all three synoptic gospels, is an important evidence of Jesus' teaching about the Holy Spirit. The occasion was the charge that Jesus cast out demons by Beelzebub, the prince of the demons. Jesus in reply not only shows the impossibility of Satan casting out Satan, but also shows the true nature of the charge as a blasphemy against the Holy Spirit. This is unforgivable, although blasphemy against Jesus Himself as Son of man (according to Matthew and Luke) may be forgiven. In no more striking way could He have brought out the sovereign character of the Spirit's work. Jesus recognized that the kind of obduracy that could attribute such beneficial results of the Spirit's work to evil agencies was beyond forgiveness.

Another aspect of the teaching of Jesus regarding the Spirit is the promise of the Spirit's guidance when the disciples have to answer for their faith (Matt. 10:19, 20; Mark 13:11). In Mark's account it occurs in the eschatological discourse, whereas in Matthew's it is in the instruction given prior to the Mission of the Twelve, but it is the kind of assurance which may well have been repeated several times. Luke has a similar statement placed in yet a different context (12:11, 12). In Luke 11:13 the Spirit is promised to those who ask the heavenly Father, and it is significant that Matthew records a parallel statement in which the promise is for "good things." Luke's account may be interpretive, but Jesus' meaning may certainly have included this aspect of the gift of the Spirit. It seems a fair interpretation that by the gift of the Spirit is to be understood the source of all "good things" which the Father is willing to bestow. Yet another comment of Jesus which illuminates the work of the Spirit is found in Mark 12:36, where Jesus attributes to the inspiration of the Spirit the statement of David in Psalm 110:1. In this Jesus shows Himself to be in line with contemporary Jewish views of inspiration.

The evidence from the fourth gospel falls naturally into two parts, the sayings before the passion narratives and the sayings within these narratives. In the discourse with Nicodemus the Spirit is shown as the agent of regeneration (John 3:5 f.). Without His activity there can be no rebirth. Whether or not there is in this chapter a reference to Christian baptism is a matter of debate, but it does not affect the essential work of the Spirit in spiritual renewal. In the same discourse in John 3, Jesus makes it clear that God does not give the Spirit by measure (v. 34), which suggests an unlimited gift. In the conversation with the Samaritan woman, Jesus speaks of the spiritual nature of God and the need for His worshipers to worship in spirit and in truth (John 4:24), and there must be seen here an allusion to the work of the Holy Spirit.

At the feast of Tabernacles Jesus promised that rivers of living waters should flow from those who come to Him, and John adds the comment that He spoke this of the Spirit. Although this is an editorial note, it is valuable as an interpretation of the imagery that Jesus used (cf. John 7:37-39).

It is in the farewell discourses in the upper room that the teaching about the Spirit becomes more explicit. There are several sayings in which the Spirit is described as the Paraclete, which is better rendered Counselor, since counselor involves the functions of both Advocate and Helper. The intercessory function, which might be suggested by Advocate is, however, lacking. The passages are John 14:16, 17, 25, 26; 15:26; 16:7-11, 13-15. In three of these passages (14:16; 15:26; 16:13) the Spirit is named as the Spirit of truth; in the first two of them, in conjunction with the word Paraclete. A summary of the function of the Holy Spirit must include the following: (a) In relation to the church, He calls to remembrance and acts as guide into the truth; (b) in relation to the world, He convicts of sin and brings recognition of the rightness of judgment. From these functions it may be deduced that the Paraclete was to continue the work of Jesus on earth. He was to be the *alter ego* of Christ. The witness of the Spirit was to be essentially the same as the witness of Christ, with the obvious further development that the Spirit would testify to the risen Christ.

The other mention of the Spirit in the teaching of Jesus occurs when He breathes upon the disciples and says, "Receive the Holy Spirit" (John 20:22). Here it is the Risen Christ who speaks and shows again the close connection between the Spirit's work and His own. The gift of the Spirit was to be given at Pentecost, but here Jesus gives His own sanction to what may be regarded as a foretaste of that event. The power to forgive and to retain sins is granted at the same time (20:23) and cannot be divorced from the activity of the Spirit. It is not incongruous with the fact that God alone forgives sins, for Jesus Himself did not hesitate to pronounce forgiveness, and the same sovereign power is vested in the Spirit and then mediately through those possessing the Spirit.

9

The Miracles of Jesus

SEPARATE CONSIDERATION IS here given to the miracles of Jesus because of their importance for a right understanding of His mission. The approach of many toward the gospel narratives is governed by their prior approach to the miracles. It is essential therefore to discuss something of their validity and character before examining their purpose.

A. The Validity of Miracles

1. *Various Approaches to Jesus' Miracles*

No one looking at the life of Jesus Christ can proceed far without being required to come to terms with His miracles. There are philosophical and scientific problems which at once arise, as a result of which many conclude for the impossibility of miracles. It is not in place here to debate this issue, but no serious investigation of the life of Jesus can pass it by. It naturally follows that those who adopt the position that miracles do not happen are obliged to explain away the miraculous elements in the gospel narratives.

During the period of nineteenth-century criticism this was done in two different ways, as was pointed out in the discussion on the various approaches to the sources for the life of Jesus. Either the miracles were rationalized and retained in the narratives or else they were discounted and consequently ignored. There is no denying that the presence of these miraculous elements was a considerable embarrassment.

During the twentieth century, however, there has been much recession of scientific skepticism regarding the possibility of miracles, although the discounting of the miracles as data for a reconstruction of the historical Jesus is still a powerful movement. Those of the Bultmann school of thought who challenge the Jesus of history find no difficulty over the miracles, for the miracle stories are considered to be creations of the primitive communities. But it should be noted that the dispensing with the miraculous in this case is part of the essentially *a priori* position of this school and does not follow from a detailed consideration of the evidence. Some who have passionately believed in the historical Jesus, as the liberal schools of the nineteenth and early twentieth centuries did, have attempted to produce lives of Jesus which lack the miraculous element, but these have more the appearance of what their authors wanted to see as the historical Jesus rather than what corresponds to historical facts. The miracles of Jesus are too baffling for those who wish to reduce everything to the level of their own experience.

The fact is that miracles are deeply imprinted on the records of the gospels, and it seems reasonable to consider them as an essential part of the over-all presentation of Jesus. The problem whether they may be regarded as actual happenings or whether they have been modified or even created in course of the transmission of the traditions is a relevant one and will be considered in the course of the general comments on the miracles of Jesus.

2. *The Classification of Miracles*

The various miracles which are attributed to Jesus may be placed into one of two categories, either healing miracles or nature miracles. The distinction is important because less difficulty is thought to attach to many of the healing miracles than to the nature miracles, mainly because they are more open to medical explanation.

Among the healing miracles a further classification has been suggested between cases of nervous disorders and other cases, because for the former modern science has methods of bringing relief which were unknown to the time of Jesus. Some conditions related in the gospels may certainly be cases where mind has dominated over matter and where the greater mind of Jesus brought physical relief. Such an explanation may be the right one in some cases, but Jesus in His miracles was infinitely more than a super-psychologist or psychiatrist. Those cases in which He concerned Himself with the sin of those who were healed shows that His main concern was spiritual. At the same time, what power the modern psychologist has is but a pale reflection of the competence with which Jesus dealt with the nervous conditions of men.

On the other hand, there are certainly some healing miracles which cannot be regarded as cases with which modern medical science could deal to bring about a similar result. A withered hand cannot be restored, nor can dead people be brought back to life after an interval of time. There is a considerable element of the inexplicable in the miracles attributed to Jesus, which in the end must either be accepted or rejected. The issue really rests on the question, "Was Jesus the kind of person who might reasonably be expected to do the inexplicable?" An attempt will be made below to give adequate reasons for an affirmative answer to this question, but before doing so some comments are necessary on the nature miracles.

Among these miracles the most notable are the draught of fishes (Luke 5:1-11; cf. John 21:1-11), the stilling of the storm (Matt. 8:26; Mark 4:37-39; Luke 8:22-24) and the feeding of the five thousand (Matt. 14:15-21; Mark 6:35-44; Luke 9:12-17; John 6:5-13). The last miracle is the only one which appears in all four gospels, a fact which fixes special attention upon it. This miracle appears to involve the operation of forces which are quite different from natural processes, while the other two are instances of control over such processes. Leaving aside for the moment the question of the purpose of these miracles in the mind of Jesus, the impact of them on the observers is beyond doubt. As a result of the draught of fishes Peter becomes overwhelmed with a sense of sinfulness, while all were afraid after the storm had abated at Jesus' command.

3. *The Characteristics of the Gospel Miracles*

Form critics have pointed out that the healing miracle stories conform to a pattern, since they contain a description of the condition, followed generally by some indication that the person desired to be healed, with some evidence of faith on the part of the healed, and this is then followed by an account of the healing, usually with some comment on the result. It is not surprising that most healing stories follow a similar pattern. But it is significant that the part played by faith is so often stressed in the synoptic gospels, although it is not mentioned in every case. The ten lepers' cry for mercy was evidently regarded as evidence of a sufficient faith-relationship (Luke 17:11 ff.), for Jesus at once proceeded to heal them. The faith element marks out Jesus as distinct from a mere wonder worker whose actions are directed toward drawing attention to Himself. That the healing miracles depended on a relationship of trust is evident from the gospels, and in this respect the miracles themselves are valuable evidence that Jesus was the kind of person who elicited trust in Himself.

The faith-element is not brought to the fore to the same extent in the fourth gospel, but it is by no means absent. The characteristic feature in this gospel is the use of the word "sign," which draws attention to the spiritual significance behind the event. More will be said on this when the purpose of the miracles is discussed, but it is again clear that none of these miracles was performed for its own sake. Throughout the accounts there is a marked restraint, and indeed on many occasions silence regarding a healing is specifically enjoined.

4. *Principles of Verification*

Due to the various source theories which have been propounded there has been a tendency to differentiate between the miracle stories on the basis of the number of witnesses which attest to any individual incident. Thus those in three or four gospels are regarded as superior to those which appear in only one or two. In this way such miracles as the coin in the fish's mouth (Matt. 17:24 f.) or the mass raisings from the tombs (Matt. 27:52 f.) are regarded as inferior. But the criterion used is not a good one, for a single witness may be as reliable as two or three. If the testimony of one witness becomes suspect in comparison with others this is a different matter, but in the instances cited this is not proved. Matthew does not heighten the miraculous when relating events also recorded by others, and in view of this there is no reason to expect that he will do so when recording unique material.

It must be assumed that all the miracles which have been preserved in the gospel tradition were evidently regarded as equally authentic. All that the modern scholar can do is to examine each individually with a view to ascertaining its probability, but this quest may be impossible since probability will depend on a prior concept of the power of Jesus. Thus this whole question of probability deserves further examination.

5. *The Probability of the Miracles*

As mentioned at the commencement of this chapter on miracles, probability may be decided on philosophical or scientific grounds. If this results in a negative conclusion, no specific discussion of the miracles of Jesus will be valid. But another and more satisfactory method, which does not in itself exclude philosophical and scientific considerations, is to view the whole matter historically and theologically. The first stage is the gospel accounts, for these testify to the strong belief on the part of the evangelists and presumably also the early church that Jesus performed such miracles. This fact raises the question of the origin of such a firm faith. If Jesus had performed no works of this character, it is difficult to believe that in such a comparatively short period so many remarkable works would have been attributed to Him. The possibility must be allowed that the early Christians created stories out of the impetus of their new-found faith in Jesus Christ, but it is incredible that they created them *ex nihilo*. The fact that they found nothing incongruous between the gospel account of the miracles and their view of Jesus suggests that their high regard for Him had some basis in historic fact. The Church's Easter faith presupposed that the historical Jesus was capable of performing miracles.

This leads to what is probably the most important consideration in any approach to miracles — the relevance of the resurrection of Christ for the inquiry. Christianity itself rests on a stupendous miracle — the raising of Christ from the dead — and it may reasonably be maintained that, if God raised Christ from the dead, the other miracles present no difficulty. The force of this position is naturally lost on those who do not regard the resurrection as historical, but as having taken place in the experience of believers (as Bultmann). If the remarkable emergence of the Christian faith in the form of a personal faith in the risen Christ is to be explained at all, it demands some explanation which adequately accounts for the totally unexpected transformation in the first Christian disciples. The actual resurrection of Christ as an objective and verifiable reality, testified to by innumerable eyewitnesses, is alone sufficient. Moreover, the evidences for the appearances of the risen Christ are so well attested that they cannot be explained away without doing injustice to the witnesses' testimony.

Granted, therefore, that the resurrection of Jesus must be regarded as an integral part of the Christian faith, it is difficult to see how lesser miracles could be treated as incongruous, unless they were out of keeping with what the gospels record about the risen Christ. But this is not true. It may be safely claimed that there is not one of the miracles which could not be conceived of as the work of Jesus. There is a complete absence of the tendency, seen all too vividly in the later church, to embellish miracle stories with fantastic details.

A further consideration is the evidence from the Temptation of Jesus, which shows His general approach to the miraculous. It is clear that self-interest was at once rejected as an unworthy motive for the performing of miracles. This is clear from the refusal to provide bread from stones, although there is an implicit assumption that Jesus had power to do so; otherwise the temptation would have been entirely unreal. Moreover, the suggestion that Jesus should throw Himself from the pinnacle of the Temple was equally refused because He did not accept the principle that miraculous power should be used for self-display. If the miracle stories are approached through the Temptation narrative, the motives behind them will not be misconstrued.

Following this reference to the Temptation, some mention must be made of the various instances of exorcisms in the gospels, for they show the close connection between many of the healing miracles and the spirit world. Some of the conditions described in the gospels may now be described in psychiatric terminology, but this does not explain away the spiritual conflict involved. Exorcism forms an important aspect of the ministry of the church, and it is inconceivable that Jesus regarded His own exorcisms as anything other than evidence of His power over the enemy. It should be noted, however, that the cases of demon possession which are recorded are not cases of excessive wickedness in the individual possessed.

The characteristic features of the condition of those possessed must have presented Jesus with a constant challenge. A primitive Church, which believed that Jesus in His death and resurrection had vanquished the power of evil, would find no difficulty in the cases of exorcisms in the gospels. It would have been more surprising if such cases had been lacking.

B. The Purpose of the Miracles

It is to the gospel of John that we must turn for a statement of the evangelist's purpose in including the "signs of Jesus." He says it is that men might "believe that Jesus is the Christ, the Son of God," but it is relevant to inquire whether Jesus Himself had a similar view. It is at once noticeable that He does not describe His own works as signs, but He does, according to John, urge men to believe His works if they cannot believe His words (John 10:38). Did He then regard His miracles as didactic, as designed to impart some spiritual truth? Some scholars have maintained this to such an extent that they have suggested that some of the stories were first parables, which in course of transmission have been transformed into miracles. The withering of the fig tree has been cited as an example. But, there is no reason why a miracle might not perform the function of a parable, without it being supposed that this accounts for its origin. In many of the events recorded some spiritual lessons are discernible, and it seems reasonable to suppose that this was part of the purpose of Jesus. The stilling of the storm, for instance, drew attention to the poverty of the disciples' faith.

Do the miracles have any bearing upon the Messianic claims of Jesus? Whatever the general expectancy that the coming Messiah would perform signs, the gospels do not give the impression that Jesus intended observers to deduce from His miracles evidence of His Messianic office. Indeed, the Temptation narrative would seem to be against any display. Miracles may be regarded as corroborating evidence for Christians who had already come to identify the risen Christ with the long awaited Jewish Messiah, but this does not appear to be a main motive for the miracles. One motive which is much stressed in the synoptic gospels is compassion. The healing miracles were often performed when a person's need awoke compassion in the Healer, and this factor draws attention to the intensely human aspect of many of the miracles. That Jesus was frequently most concerned with this aspect is seen from the fact that silence was sometimes immediately enjoined. A few acts of compassion could otherwise easily have grown into a mass ministry of healing, which Jesus clearly avoided, because it would deflect Him from His main redemptive purpose.

The most important thing about the miracles is what one learns from them about Jesus Himself. The element of restraint is self-evident. The miracles are samples of a power which belonged to the nature of Jesus, and His refraining from using that power is on occasions more eloquent than its use. He could have commanded more than twelve legions of angels (Matt. 26:53) to come to His aid, but this exercise of power would have run counter to the purpose of His mission. Indeed, it is here that the key to an understanding of the miracles is to be found, for Jesus had one dominating purpose – to fulfill the Father's will. This is brought out more clearly in John's gospel than elsewhere, but it is of utmost importance. He did not regard any of His works as His own. They were the Father's works. They are evidences, therefore, of the Father's pleasure in the Son, and are accordingly a witness to His divine claims.

The miracles may be incredible as works of a man, however perfect, but new possibilities are opened up when the man concerned, not only claimed to be Son of God, but was acknowledged to be so by the early Christians.

10

Jesus Christ in Early Christian Thought

It does not lie within the scope of this book to give a full discussion of Christological problems, but no account of Jesus Christ would be complete that failed to consider the place He gained in the theology of the developing church. For this reason a brief survey will be given of the different though complementary lines of approach found in the various New Testament books.

A. Primitive Thought

First to be considered must be the view of Jesus found in the primitive *Kerygma* (the content of preaching), the sources for which are the early Acts speeches and some earlier traditional material taken over by Paul. To this must be added any data that can be deduced from the manner in which the evangelists commented on their materials. That Jesus Christ immediately became the center of the church's proclamation is not only an undeniable fact, but in the nature of the case could not have been otherwise. It was His resurrection which transformed the tragedy of the cross into a triumph. The church was founded on the fact that Jesus was not dead, but alive.

Various titles are used of Jesus in the speeches in Acts which reveal what the early Christians understood of the nature of His mission. He is certainly identified as the Messiah (Christ), as is clear from Peter's first sermon (Acts 2:36), where the messiahship is linked with lordship. This shows a remarkable penetration into the real nature of Jesus of Nazareth, which was basic to all primitive Christian theology. The human Jesus is now the exalted Lord. For a further clear identification of Jesus as the Christ, cf. Acts 3:20; 4:10; 5:42; 8:5.

More distinctive of the Acts speeches are the titles "Servant" and "Prince of Life." The former connects Jesus with the Servant passages of Isaiah, and it seems reasonable to suggest that the early Christians made this identification on the strength of the marked similarity between Isaiah 53 and the death of Jesus. Some have disputed this identification as an element in primitive theology (e.g. M. D. Hooker, *Jesus and the Servant* [1959]), but it cannot be excised from all the streams of early Christian thought where it appears. It occurs in Acts 3:13, 26; 4:27. In the first two occurrences it is God who takes the part of the Servant and exalts him. This Servant concept played an important part in the primitive interpretation of the death of Christ, and also supplied a powerful example for Christians under trial (cf. I Peter 2:21 ff.). The description of Jesus as Prince of Life (or Author of Life, Acts 3:15) brings out the fact that He is for the Christians the dispenser of Life, i.e., Life as understood in a new way, Life dominated by the power of the risen Christ. Stephen in his defense before the Sanhedrin, introduces Jesus under the name of the Righteous One (7:52), which must be understood as a confession of the sinless character of Jesus. It is noteworthy that in neither of the mission speeches of Paul recorded in Acts does Paul use any specific title for Jesus other than "Savior" in 13:23, which even then is more a description than a title.

Although interest in the historical life of Jesus is overshadowed by the dominant focus upon the resurrection, such references are not entirely lacking. Peter's speech to Cornelius is of the greatest importance (Acts 10:37 ff.). This shows interest in Jesus' preaching ministry in Galilee and Judea, in His endowment with the Spirit (understood as a divine anointing – evidently at His baptism by John), in His works of healing and exorcism, and in His death and resurrection. The exalted Lord was none other than the Jesus of Nazareth, whose doings and words could be recalled by those who saw and heard them.

From the speeches in Acts may be deduced not only the exalted concept of Jesus Christ which was held by the earlier believers, but also the fact that on the basis of His death and resurrection salvation could now be offered to all who would repent and believe in him (cf. 2:38, 39; 3:19, 25, 26; 4:12; 5:14). Jesus Christ had become the key to the divine offer of forgiveness. Moreover, the Holy Spirit's activity is inseparably connected with the continuing activity of Jesus in His Church (cf. 2:33; 5:32).

In the editorial sections of the gospels, a similar exalted concept of Jesus is seen. Matthew and Luke, for instance, in their different ways include supernatural elements in the birth story. Mark begins his gospel with a description of Jesus as Son of God (Mark 1:1). In Matthew and to a lesser extent in Mark and Luke the coming of Jesus is set against the background of Old Testament prophecy. The evangelists never thought of Jesus except as the One foreshadowed by the prophets. Both Matthew and Mark make it clear that the dynamic works of Jesus were restricted through unbelief (Matt. 13:58; Mark 6:5), showing how the incarnation was in some ways conditioned by man's response.

The *Kerygma* is seen in the works of Paul in those sections where he is indebted to others for the tradition. The most notable passage is I Corinthians 15:3 ff., in which certain facts about Christ are said to have been received. These include the fact of His death and its interpretation as "for our sins," the fact of His burial, the fact of the resurrection on the third day and of His appearances to various people, many of them named witnesses. It is clear, therefore, that while Paul is not unmindful of the importance of the facts, he is more interested in their significance, and this becomes most evident in his own distinctive Christology.

Before considering this, reference must be made to two other Scripture sections singled out by C. H. Dodd in his *Apostolic Preaching and Its Developments* as belonging to the primitive *Kerygma*. Romans 10:9 presents a primitive confession of faith – Jesus is Lord. Since this confession is said to be sufficient for salvation, the idea of the Lordship of Christ must have possessed wide connotation. Indeed, this confession cannot be placed over against the statement that Jesus is Christ, as a Greek creed over against a Jewish (as Bousset maintained), for Paul's doctrine shows a combination of the two. Dodd also sees Romans 1:1-4 as a possible early Christian creedal statement; if this is true it shows the recognition of His Davidic descent, of His Sonship, of the powerful effects of the resurrection and of His messiahship and Lordship. All these features are fully developed by the apostle in his doctrinal teaching.

B. Pauline Thought

1. *Preliminary Observations*

The history of criticism shows that Paul has often been accused of imposing upon the primitive Gospel his own concepts of Jesus Christ. For this reason it is essential to recognize the unity of Paul's view of Jesus Christ with that of the primitive community and, indeed, with that taught by Jesus concerning Himself. Some of the earlier critics, such as F. C. Baur, maintained that Paul's concept of Christ was directly due to his logical processes of mind. This theory failed because it did not take sufficiently into account the objective reality of Paul's Damascus road experience. More recent interpreters of Paul have regarded his Christology as a Hellenization of Christianity, a process which is also claimed for Johannine Christology. Again, the thoroughly Jewish character of some of Paul's fundamental concepts (e.g., his concept of righteousness) cannot be so explained. The same goes for supposed pagan influences upon Paul's mind (as in Bultmann's theory of the redeemer myth and the heavenly man). Quite apart from the fact that supporting evidence is much too late to be valid for the period of Paul's ministry, the claim that Christianity was mixed in Paul's mind with such pagan myths would require indubitable evidence to substantiate it. Probability is heavily weighted against it. It is more credible to see Paul's view of Christ as a development of what was inherently present in the primitive ideas.

Attention has already been drawn to the apostle's knowledge of the earthly life of Jesus. This must presuppose that he accepted some connection between the historic Jesus and the Jesus who met him on the Damascus road. His experience at that time confirmed the activity of the risen Lord in the experience of his people. It was essentially Christ, not the Christians, who was the object of Paul's persecuting zeal, a realization which may well have caused him to ponder the indwelling of Christ in His people through the Spirit, which became a cardinal feature of His Christology. There can be no doubt that in Paul's case he did not begin with detailed knowledge of the historical Jesus and then work up toward an exalted Christology. It was the risen Christ who arrested him in his religious quest and it was the risen Christ who dominated his theology. There is no evidence in his epistles that it was immaterial to him whether the Jesus of the Damascus road was the same Jesus who lived and died on a cross in Palestine. His Christology makes sense only if such an identification is assumed.

2. *Summary of Paul's Christology*

A brief summary of the main elements in Paul's own special understanding of Christ is needed to set the historical Jesus firmly in the faith of the Christian church.

a. *The New Adam.* Paul is deeply conscious of the need of man, summarized in the failure of the first Adam with its consequent disastrous effects on the whole race (Rom. 5:12 ff.). He sees, however, in Christ the head of a new race as Adam was of the old. The contrast is striking, for whereas Adam is believed to be carnal, Christ is seen as spiritual, and whereas Adam could only bring death, Christ brings life. There is no need to look to non-Jewish ideas of a heavenly man, although some parallels may exist. It is sufficient to see in this concept of the apostle a development from the comparison of the old order with the new.

b. *The Pre-existent Christ.* There are certain indications that Paul accepted the pre-existence of Christ. It was in the fulness of time that God sent forth His Son (Gal. 4:4). It is possible that when Paul identified the Rock which followed the children of Israel as being Christ (I Cor. 10:4), he was thinking of the existence of Christ in the period of the wilderness wanderings. When the apostle refers in II Corinthians 8:9 to the fact that though Christ was rich yet He became poor for our sakes, there may be the suggestion of a voluntary act. There is no denying this in the great Christological passage of Philippians 2:5-11. This passage, with its concept of Christ not grasping at equality with God, but humbling Himself to the death of the cross, shows the profound understanding which the apostle had of the incarnation. Even if it be maintained that Paul is using an existing hymn to Christ, his use of it shows his own endorsement of this conception of Christ. The idea of Christ's pre-existence does not, however, depend on a few passages, but is basic to Paul's Christology. It is directly connected with his idea of the cosmic significance of Christ.

c. *Cosmic Significance.* The major statement concerning this is found in Colossians 1:15-20, where Paul shows Christ as (1) Instrument in Creation, (2) Sustainer of all, and (3) Goal of all. This shows an extension to the cosmic realm of Paul's understanding of the death and resurrection of Christ in the spiritual and moral realm. His superiority in the one implies His superiority in the other. He who is Head of the Church is Head of the created order. It is important to note that the creatorship of Christ is not dwelt upon for its own sake, but for its essential part in the whole scheme of redemption. The one in whom men have forgiveness of sins is the same one in whom the fulness of God dwells. Such a Christology seems far removed from the historical Jesus, but there is nothing in the developed Christology of Paul which could not have come from the essential character of Jesus as seen in the gospels. An earlier passage in I Corinthians 8:6, adumbrated something of the same thought. While there are certain parallels of language between Paul's cosmic view of Christ and Greek speculative thought, His concept is unique for Christ as agent in creation is also Redeemer and Head of His people. Again, the idea of wisdom personified in Jewish Wisdom literature (e.g. Prov. 8:22, 23, 29, 30; Wisd. Sol. 9:2) supplies certain parallels, but Paul's concept is not a personification but a person. In viewing the created world he sees all things summed up in one person, Christ (Eph. 1:10) as the perfect expression of the mind of God.

d. *Relationship With the Father.* Some passages in Paul's epistles suggest the subordination of Christ to the Father, but these must be understood by a direct comparison with the statements of Jesus. The Son is sent by God (Gal. 4:4). It is God who highly exalted Him (Phil. 2:9). He will deliver up the Kingdom to the Father (I Cor. 15:28). The idea that God spared not His own Son (Rom. 8:32) may also suggest the same idea. There is much that is akin to the teaching of Jesus about Himself in the fourth gospel, especially the constantly reiterated theme of His being sent to do the will of the Father. Jesus was speaking in a historical context, and it is equally clear that Paul is thinking of Him in such a context rather than stating an absolute truth.

e. *Relationship With the Spirit.* According to Paul, there is an indissoluble union between Christ and the Spirit, as there is between Christ and the Father. So close is it that some, on the strength of II Corinthians 3:17, have suggested the idea of identity, but when Paul speaks of the Spirit of the Lord, a distinction is in mind. There is a close affinity between his concept here and that found in Acts, where the work of the Spirit and the continuing work of Jesus in His Church are essentially related.

It will be seen that Paul's view of Christ is inseparably linked with the historical Jesus who is everywhere assumed, and reaches out toward a full-orbed concept of Him in harmony with the revelation of the Easter event. The resurrection did not make Jesus what He was not before in His essence, but it did reveal His true nature and released divine power for salvation.

C. Johannine Thought

The teaching of Jesus about Himself in the fourth gospel has already been mentioned, but there are features in the presentation of Jesus by John in this gospel which throw light on early Christology. The most significant is the Logos doctrine in the Prologue (John 1:1-18). The choice of such an opening is illuminating by way of comparison with the synoptic gospels. It at once draws attention to the pre-existence of Christ, to His creatorship, and to His Godhead. What the origin is of the term Logos, used in this sense, is not of vital importance for our present purpose, for it is the characteristics rather than the origin, of the Logos which reveal John's concept of Christ. Unlike Philo's Logos, John's Logos reaches his fulfillment in incarnation (1:14). Since, after mentioning this, John does not again refer to the Logos, it cannot be regarded as the key for the understanding of his gospel. Nevertheless, in his account of the historical Jesus, he does not intend the reader to be unaware that this Jesus possessed a divine nature. He never thought of his narrative as the record of a man, however perfect, but as the record of the eternal Son of God in human form.

The stated purpose of the Gospel in John 20:30, 31 must be noted, for it shows not only John's evangelical purpose, but also his essential view of Christ. "That you may believe that Jesus is the Christ, the Son of God" reveals a double aspect of His person. His messiahship and His divine Sonship are reckoned to shine through His words and works. To John, Jesus is nothing less than "the only Son, who is in the bosom of the Father" (1:18). That this means that John's account is theological in purpose rather than historical cannot be denied, but this does not mean that the history was unimportant. John's whole purpose is, in fact, to show the entry of the divine into history. It has earlier been mentioned that John records more specific examples of the real humanity of Jesus than the synoptics. He is wearied with travel, suffers thirst (John 4), expresses strong indignation (cf. John 11:33, 38), and weeps (John 11:35).

The Johannine epistles share the same exalted view of Christ as the fourth gospel. His Sonship is frequently stressed. He is called our Advocate (I John 2:1) and is named as Jesus the righteous. His Messiahship is insisted upon (I John 2:22; 4:2; 5:1) in such a way as to exclude any Docetic notion of drawing a distinction between Jesus and the Christ. He is moreover named as Savior of the world (I John 4:14). Indeed, there is much in I John which echoes the language and ideas of John's gospel and shows that both books share the same Christological viewpoint. II John reflects the same position as I John (cf. II John 7:9).

In the Apocalypse a further aspect of Christology is seen. The central figure is the Lamb, who is a slain yet triumphant figure. The link with the historical Jesus is unmistakable, but the Lamb's exaltation shows His commanding position in the cosmic drama. Although many setbacks come to God's people, there is never any doubt about the ultimate result. The most dominant factor is that the Lamb has become the Judge to execute judgment upon those opposed to the divine will. This aspect is seen in the writer's vision of the one like the Son of man in the midst of the candlesticks (Rev. 1:12-16). From His mouth there issued a sword, in his hand were securely held the stars which represented his people. It is important to note that the name he bears at the moment of judgment is "The Word of God" (Rev. 19:13), which provides a direct link with the prologue of John's gospel. He is, moreover, King of kings and Lord of lords, the Alpha and the Omega, all titles which suggest the sovereignty of the Lamb.

D. Other Aspects of Christ

In the epistle to the Hebrews, the most characteristic concept of Jesus is that of High Priest, which controls the development of the argument of the whole epistle. The new revelation which has come in Christ marks Him out as superior to the prophets (Heb. 1:1), to Moses (Heb. 3:1 ff.) and to Aaron (Heb. 5:1 ff.). He belongs to a new order, that of Melchizedek, which nevertheless is essentially a priestly order. The writer sets the tone for his letter in Hebrews 1:2, 3, where he reveals his exalted concept of Christ as heir and creator of all things, and bearing the very stamp of God's nature. He could not have expressed more vividly the absolute sovereignty of Christ, and yet he links with this the fact that He has purged man's sins. The inseparable connection between the historical act of redemption and the present exalted position of Christ is inescapable. This is borne out by the references in the epistle to aspects of the earthly experience of Jesus: His temporarily inferior position to the angels, His condescension to suffering and death (2:9), His subjection to temptation (2:18), His faithfulness (3:6), His agonizing prayers (5:7), the specific reference to "the days of his flesh" (5:7), and His determination to do God's will (10:5-7).

The mission of Jesus historically is viewed in sacrificial terms. The difference between the offering of Jesus and the offerings of the Aaronic order rested in the character of both offering and offerer. The perfection of Christ insured the complete adequacy of His offering. This interpretation of the work of Christ shows the exalted concept of His character which the writer held. His exposition is also valuable because it draws attention to the present mission of Jesus in His exalted position. It is a ministry of intercession (4:15; 7:25). There is a constant representative of man at the right hand of God, who, in spite of the fact that He is a consuming fire (12:29), is nevertheless a God of mercy (4:16).

Another view of Christ brought to the fore in Hebrews is that of Ratifier of the New Covenant (8:6 ff.; 9:1 ff.). Because of the inadequacy of the Old Covenant, the inauguration of the New was of vital concern to mankind. What Jesus Himself foreshadowed at the institution of the Lord's Supper, the writer to the Hebrews develops. Here is seen the fulfillment of Jeremiah's prophecy (Jer. 31, cf. Heb. 8:8), which emphasizes the essential inwardness of the New as contrasted with the Old. In this is shown once again the superiority of Christ over Moses, and, *ipso facto*, the superiority of Christianity over Judaism.

In I Peter the Christology conforms to a pattern similar to the other streams of thought already mentioned. There is awareness, on the one hand, of the human aspect of the character of Jesus Christ, for He is said to have left man an example to follow in His steps. This must mean a concentration on the historical Jesus, whose sufferings in order to form an example for believers must be of the same kind as theirs. The uniqueness of His sufferings lies in the fact that he bore man's sins (I Pet. 2:24; 4:18). He is called Shepherd (2:25; 5:4) and Guardian (2:25), both of which titles stress His special care for His people. The Lordship of Christ is assumed (cf. I Pet. 1:3; 3:15, 21, 22). His role as Redeemer of His people is particularly brought out by means of the Servant passage in 2:21 ff., by the allusions to the Exodus passage in 1:13 ff., and by the frequent reference to His sufferings.

There are undoubtedly affinities between the Christology of I Peter and that of Paul. It is quite unnecessary to suppose that in all these relationships, Peter is dependent on Paul, for most are basic to the primitive *Kerygma.* Both Peter and Paul develop these basic concepts in their own way. It is possible that th affinities between I Peter and Romans and Ephesians may be du to literary influences. But it is certain, whatever the decision c that matter may be, that both apostles held the same exalted vie of Christ and the same conviction about the continuity betwe this concept and the historic Jesus. The most individualistic fe ture in Peter's Christology is his reference to the descent of Chri into Hades, presumably in the interval between His death ar resurrection (3:18 f.). Whatever the precise explanation of th difficult statement, it is evident that Peter conceived of an exte sion of the preaching ministry of Jesus even after His death.

In II Peter Jesus Christ is named as Savior (II Peter 1:1) an as Lord (1:2; cf. also 1:8, 11; 2:20; 3:2, 18). His majesty i specially mentioned which leads to a specific reference to th Transfiguration (1:16 f.). Another allusion is to the Master wh bought them (2:1), a clear reference to the redemptive activity of Christ as in I Peter 1. Although far less developed in its Christology as compared with I Peter, this epistle is nonetheless in line with the general primitive position.

James is remarkably sparse in its references to Christ, the only specific instances being in James 1:1 and 2:1. In both of these He is called the Lord Jesus Christ, and in the latter also the Lord of glory. Yet this is not the extent of the witness of this epistle to Christ. There are more echoes of the sayings of Jesus in this epistle than in any other New Testament book, particularly from the Sermon on the Mount. It may be inferred that James knew much of the historical Jesus, but he nonetheless conceived Him to be the Lord of glory. If his interests are mainly ethical in this epistle, this is no criterion for supposing that the two references to Christ are the total extent of his Christological understanding.

The brief epistle of Jude shares a Christology similar to II Peter. Christ is Master and Lord (v. 4) and the same title Lord Jesus Christ is used three times (vv. 17, 21, 25).

E. Conclusion

However many-sided the views of the early Christians regarding Jesus, there is a basic oneness throughout. Jesus is more than a figure of history, although He is that. He is the exalted Lord whose power ranges over the whole created order, but He holds a special relationship to His Church.

Bibliography

In the following lists a representative selection has been made of titles not already mentioned in the book. The lists are arranged for convenience under the separate chapters to which they mainly refer, in order of date of publication.

Chapter 2. The Background to the Life of Jesus

Schurer, E. *History of the Jewish People in the Time of Jesus Christ.* T & T Clark (1890-91).
Although an older work, a valuable survey of the history and literature of the pre-Christian period. Needs supplementing by more recent works.

Oesterley, W. O. E. & Box, G. H. *The Religion and Worship of the Synagogue,* Pitman (1911).
A treatment of Jewish worship procedures.

Bevan, E. E., editor. *Hellenism and Christianity.* Allen & Unwin (1921).
Valuable essays on the Greek background of the period.

Strack, H. L. & Billerbeck, P. *Kommentar zum Neue Testament aus Talmud und Midrash.* Beck (1922-1928).
A valuable source book on the Jewish background.

Herford, R. T. *The Pharisees.* Allen & Unwin (1924).
A standard work on the Pharisees.

Halliday, W. R. *The Pagan Background of Early Christianity.* Hodder & Stoughton (1925).
An older book which still contains much of value.

Moore, G. F. *Judaism.* Harvard U. P. (1927-30).
A three-volume very full work, weakened by overemphasis on later sources for first century Judaism.

Tarn, W. W. *The Hellenistic Civilization.* Arnold (1927). 3rd edition (1952).
A useful survey of Greek culture from the time of Alexander the Great to A.D. 30.

Finklestein, L. *The Pharisees.* Jewish Publication Society of America (1938).
A Jewish account of the subject.

Jocz, J. *The Jewish People and Jesus Christ.* S. P. C. K. (1949).
A useful comparison between the teaching of Judaism and the teaching of Jesus.

Filson, F. V. *The New Testament Against Its Environment.* S. C. M. (1950).
A survey of the many facets which go to make up the background of early Christianity.

Johnson, S. E. *Jesus in His Own Times.* Black (1957).
A study of the contemporary movements, especially the revolutionaries.

Bruce, F. F. *Second Thoughts on the Dead Sea Scrolls.* Paternoster (1960).
An authoritative treatment of the subject.

Grant, F. C. *Ancient Judaism and the New Testament.* Oliver & Boyd (1960).
An attempt to smooth over the historical conflict between Judaism and early Christianity.

Russell, D. S. *Between the Testaments.* S. C. M. (1960).
An up-to-date treatment of the inter-testamental literature.

Dupont-Sumner, A. *Essene Writings From Qumran.* Blackwell (1960).
A useful introduction to the scrolls.

Tenney M. C. *New Testament Survey.* Eerdmans (1961).
A good introduction to background and literature.

Davies, W. D. *Christian Origins and Judaism.* Darton, Longman & Todd (1962).
Brings out the basically Jewish background to New Testament thought.

Grant, F. C. *Roman Hellenism and the New Testament.* Oliver & Boyd (1962).

Examines the Hellenistic background, but often finds it in the New Testament where others do not.

Filson, F. V. *A New Testament History.* S. C. M. (1964).
A useful presentation of the historical sequence of events.

Forster, W. *Palestinian Judaism in New Testament Times.* Oliver & Boyd (1964).
Valuable survey of the history of Judaism in the inter-testamental and early Christian times.

Tenney, M. C. *New Testament Times.* Eerdmans-Tyndale (1965).
A valuable background book for the New Testament.

Chapters 3 and 4. Approaches and Literary Sources

Lightfoot, R. H. *Locality and Doctrine in the Gospels.* Hodder & Stoughton (1938).
A rather radical form critical approach.

Taylor, V. *The Gospels.* Epworth. 5th edition (1945).
Brief survey of introductory material from a source critical point of view.

Huck, A. & Lietzmann, H. *Synopsis of the First Three Gospels.* Blackwell. 9th edition (1949).
A standard synopsis of the Synoptic Gospels in the Greek text. Invaluable for comparing parallel passages.

Butler, B. C. *The Originality of Matthew.* Cambridge U. P. (1951).
A Roman Catholic attempt to defend the tradition that Matthew's Gospel was the source of Mark's.

Henderson, I. *Myth in the New Testament.* S. C. M. (1952).
An acute critique of Bultmann's theory of demythologization.

Knox, W. L. *Sources of the Synoptic Tradition.* Cambridge U. P. (I 1953, II 1957).
A classical example of a source critical approach to the gospels.

McNeile, A. H. & Williams, C. S. C. *Introduction to the New Testament.* Oxford U. P. 2nd edition (1953).
For many years a standard textbook from a non-conservative point of view. Now rather dated.

Howard, W. F. & Barrett, C. K. *The Fourth Gospel in Recent Criticism.* Epworth (1955).
A useful survey of various theories about the fourth gospel, treated historically. Better on the earlier than the later period.

Hughes, P. E. *Scripture and Myth.* Tyndale (1956).
A study from a conservative point of view.

Dunkerly, R. *Beyond the Gospels.* Penguin (1957).
A collection of evidences for the life of Christ and His sayings from sources outside the Gospels.

Jeremias, J. *Unknown Sayings of Jesus.* S. P. C. K. (1957).
A collection of the non-canonical sayings of Jesus.

Bultmann, R. *Jesus Christ and Mythology.* S. C. M. (1958).
An exposition of radical demythologization theories.

Grant, R. M. & Freedman, D. N. *The Secret Sayings of Jesus.*
A study of Gnostic sayings attributed to Jesus. Useful for a comparison with the canonical sayings.

Higgins, A. J. B. *The Historicity of the Fourth Gospel.* Lutterworth (1960).
A careful study of John's historicity. Moderate in viewpoint.

Moule, C. F. D. *The Birth of the New Testament.* Black (1962).
A survey of literary development from a moderate form critical position.

Wilson, R. M. *Studies in the Gospel of Thomas.* Mowbray (1962).
An authoritative work on this recently discovered book.

Beare, F. W. *The Earliest Records of Jesus.* Blackwell (1962).
A study from a source critical point of view based on Huck's *Synopsis.*

Feine, P., Behm, J., Kummel, W. G. *Einleitung in das Neue Testament.* Quelle & Meyer (1963). English edition, *Introduction to the New Testament,* S. C. M. (1968).
Best modern New Testament Introduction from a non-conservative. Valuable for bibliography.

Grant, R. M. *A Historical Introduction to the New Testament.* Collins (1963).
A work from a liberal scholar which surprisingly often supports moderately conservative conclusions.

Hennecke, E. & Wilson, R. M. *New Testament Apocrypha I.* Lutterworth (1963).
An authoritative collection and translation of the apocryphal New Testament books. Translated and revised from the German by R. M. Wilson.

Stonehouse, N. B. *Origins of the Synoptic Gospels.* Eerdmans-Tyndale (1963).
Valuable essays on the Synoptic problem from a conservative scholar.

Braaten, C. E. & Harrisville, R. A. *The Historical Jesus and the Kerygmatic Christ.* Abingdon (1964).
Essays written from the form critical point of view.

Harrison, E. F. *Introduction to the New Testament.* Eerdmans (1964).
A good general conservative introduction.

Sparks, H. F. D. *A Synopsis of the Gospels.* Black (1964).
A useful synopsis of the Synoptic Gospels in the Revised Version English text.

Guthrie, D. *New Testament Introduction: The Gospels and Acts.* Tyndale (1965). Now published as part of a revised one volume *New Testament Introduction.* Tyndale (1970).
A more detailed examination of introductory problems.

Fuller, D. P. *Easter Faith and History.* Eerdmans-Tyndale (1965).
An excellent survey of the various critical approaches to the resurrection of Jesus.

Barclay, W. *The First Three Gospels.* S. C. M. (1966).
A fairly detailed account of critical views on the origin of these gospels and a study of each individually.

Fuller, R. H. *A Critical Introduction to the New Testament.* Duckworth (1966).
A concise account of critical theories. Assumes critical conclusions without sufficient discussion.

Hanson, A. T., editor. *Vindications.* S. C. M. (1966).
Some useful essays critical of some of the assumptions of form criticism.

Rohde, J. *Rediscovering the Teaching of the Evangelists.* S. C. M. (1966.)
A valuable survey of the most important German advocates of theological editing in the gospels. Little attempt to assess them.

Barrett, C. K. *Jesus and the Gospel Tradition.* S. P. C. K. (1967).
A liberal scholar's attempt to define the relation of Jesus to the Christian tradition.

Brandon, S. G. F. *Jesus and the Zealots.* Scribners (1967).
A radical theory that Jesus was associated with a revolutionary movement.

Betz, O. *What Do We Know About Jesus?* Westminster (1968).
A very brief survey of the current debate.

Cullmann, O. *The New Testament.* S. C. M. (1968).
A popular presentation of introductory matter by a well-known New Testament scholar.

Hunter, A. M. *According to John.* S. C. M. (1968).
A useful brief presentation of the problems concerning this gospel.

Martyn, J. L. *History and Theology in the Fourth Gospel.* Harper (1968).
Weighted toward a theological interpretation, which treats the events as both actual and symbolical.

Barker, G. W., Lane, W. L., Michaels, J. R. *The New Testament Speaks.* Harper (1969).
A good general introductory work on the New Testament.

Benoit, P. *The Passion and Resurrection of Jesus Christ.* Darton, Longman & Todd (1969).
A liberal Roman Catholic treatment of the accounts, historical and non-technical.

Chapters 5 - 7. LIFE AND MINISTRY OF JESUS

Sanday, W. *The Life of Christ in Recent Research.* Oxford U. P. (1907).
A useful survey of discussions at the close of the nineteenth century.

Seeley, J. *Ecce Homo.* Dent (1908).
A standard liberal life of Jesus.

Williams, A. L. *The Hebrew-Christian Messiah.* S. P. C. K. (1916).
A collection of lectures on Jesus from a Jewish Christian point of view.

Glover, T. R. *The Jesus of History.* S. C. M. (1920).
An essentially liberal approach to the historical Jesus.

Papini, G. *The Story of Jesus.* Hodder & Stoughton (1923).
A modern novelistic treatment.

Sanday, W. *Outlines of the Life of Jesus.* T & T Clark (1925).
An adaptation of an article in Hastings' *Dictionary of the Bible.* A generally conservative approach to the historical Jesus.

Klausner, J. *Jesus of Nazareth.* Allen & Unwin. 2nd edition (1929).
A Jewish and generally hostile approach to the life of Jesus.

Goguel, M. *Life of Jesus.* Allen & Unwin (1933).
A critical treatment which reaches many conclusions adverse to the historicity.

Sutcliffe, E. F. *A Two-Year Public Ministry.* Burns & Oates (1938).
A chronological study based on a two-year scheme.

Ogg, G. *A Chronology of the Public Ministry of Jesus.* Cambridge U. P. (1940).
A detailed discussion of the problems, which concludes that John's account is irreconcilable with the Synoptics.

Rawlinson, A. E. J. *Christ in the Gospels.* Oxford U. P. (1944).
A useful account of the Christology of the Gospels.

Dibelius, M. *Jesus.* Westminster (1949). S. C. M. (1963).
An account of Jesus from a form critical point of view.

Hunter, A. M. *The Work and Words of Jesus.* S. C. M. (1950).
A concise and readable treatment of the main features of Jesus' life.

Turner, H. E. W. *Jesus, Master and Lord.* Mowbray (1953).
A modern positive assessment of the problems in approaching the historical Jesus.

Taylor, V. *The Life and Ministry of Jesus.* Macmillan (1955).
An attempt from a moderately critical viewpoint to deal with the main events and teaching.

Fuller, R. H. *The Mission and Achievement of Jesus.* S. C. M. 2nd edition (1956).
A study from the side of form criticism.

Stauffer, E. *Jesus and His Story.* S. C. M. (1960).
A German attempt to reinstate the Jesus of History.

Hebert, G. *The Christ of Faith and the Jesus of History.* S. C. M. (1962).
Presents a view of Jesus under the New Quest.

Foster, R. C. *Studies in the Life of Christ.* 3 vols. Baker (1962-68).

A strongly conservative approach to the life of Christ.

Chapters 8 and 9. THE TEACHING AND MIRACLES OF JESUS

Denney, J. *Jesus and the Gospel.* Hodder & Stoughton (1909).
An older book that contains much valuable discussion.

Montefiore, C. G. *Rabbinic Literature and Gospel Teachings.* Macmillan (1930).
A Jewish approach to the gospels, critical and provocative.

Dodd, C. H. *The Parables of the Kingdom.* Nisbet (1935).
An interpretation of the parables from a critical point of view, with emphasis on eschatology.

Richardson, A. *Miracle Stories of the Gospels.* S. C. M. 2nd edition (1942).
An attempt to bring out the significance of these stories. Critical, but not so skeptical as some.

Curtis, W. A. *Jesus Christ the Teacher.* Oxford U. P. (1943).
A special study of the teaching of Jesus, mainly from the Synoptic Gospels.

Taylor, V. *Jesus and His Sacrifice.* Macmillan (1943).
A study of the teaching of Jesus on the atonement.

Kummel, W. G. *Promise and Fulfilment.* S. C. M. (1955).
A survey of the fulfillment idea in the New Testament.

Wilder, A. N. *New Testament Faith for Today.* S. C. M. (1956).
A study of various aspects of New Testament thought.

Stewart, J. S. *The Life and Teaching of Jesus Christ.* Church of Scotland. 2nd edition (1958).
A good general treatment in a readable style.

Ladd, G. E. *The Gospel of the Kingdom.* Harper & Row (1959).
A detailed examination of New Testament teaching. One of the best treatments from a conservative point of view.

Hunter, A. M. *Interpreting the Parables.* S. C. M. (1960).
A valuable introductory study of the parables.

Ridderbos, H. *The Coming of the Kingdom.* Presbyterian & Reformed Publishing Co. (1962).
Another thorough treatment of Kingdom teaching from a constructive standpoint.

Baird, J. A. *The Justice of God in the Teaching of Jesus.* Westminster (1963).
A useful survey of an important aspect of New Testament teaching.

Jeremias, J. *On the Parables.* S. C. M. (1963).
A study of the parables based on a form critical approach.

Flew, R. N. *Jesus and His Way.* Epworth (1963).
A study of New Testament ethics.

Fuller, R. H. *Interpreting the Miracles.* S. C. M. (1963).
A modern approach to the subject.

Marshall, I. H. *Eschatology and the Parables.* Tyndale (1963).
A brief but valuable examination of the eschatological interpretation of the parables.

Davies, W. D. *The Setting of the Sermon on the Mount.* Cambridge U. P. (1964).
A very full examination of Matthew 5 - 7. The sermon is regarded as a compilation comprising a Christian Mishna.

Loos, H. van der. *The Miracles of Jesus.* Brill (1965).
A basic examination of the miracles. Very detailed, but valuable for those making a special study of the subject.

Lunnemann, E. *Parables of Jesus.* S. P. C. K. (1966).
A general introduction with a special study of selected parables. A moderately critical work.

Chapter 10. JESUS CHRIST IN EARLY CHRISTIAN THOUGHT.

Liddon, H. P. *The Divinity of Our Lord.* Rivingtons (1866).
For more than a century a standard work on the subject.
Warfield, B. B. *The Lord of Glory.* Hodder & Stoughton (1907).
A solid examination of the Biblical evidence.
Denney, J. *Jesus and the Gospel.* Hodder & Stoughton. 2nd edition (1909).
A careful work, conservative in approach.
Forsyth, P. T. *The Person and Place of Jesus Christ.* Independent (1909).
Contains much suggestive material.
Mackintosh, H. R. *The Doctrine of the Person of Jesus Christ.* T & T Clark. 3rd edition (1914).
A standard work on this doctrine.
Kennedy, H. A. A. *The Theology of the Epistles.* Duckworth (1919).
A useful brief survey of the theology, bringing out its unity.
Rawlinson, A. E. J. *The New Testament Doctrine of the Christ.* Longmans (1926).
A standard work on New Testament Christology.
Scott, C. A. A. *Christianity According to St. Paul.* Cambridge U. P. (1927).
An examination of the main themes of Paul's theology.
Brunner, E. *The Mediator.* Lutterworth (1934).
A study of the Atonement from a dialectical viewpoint.
Bultmann, R. *Jesus and the Word.* Nicholson & Watson (1935).
Bultmann's first exposition of his Christ of Faith theology.
Howard, W. F. *Christianity According to St. John.* Duckworth (1943).
A survey of the various strands of Johannine theology.
Baillie, D. *God Was in Christ.* Faber (1948).
An incisive treatment of the doctrine of the person of Christ.
Grant, F. C. *Introduction to New Testament Thought.* Abingdon (1950).
An approach to New Testament theology from a liberal viewpoint.
Warfield, B. B. *The Person and Work of Christ.* Presbyterian & Reformed (1950).
A reprint of an older, but valuable discussion from a conservative author.
Stauffer, E. *New Testament Theology.* S. C. M. (1955).
Much useful material, although basically critical.
Bultmann, R. *Theology of the New Testament.* S. C. M. (1956).
A radical approach which pays little attention to the teaching of Jesus.
Filson, F. V. *Jesus Christ the Risen Lord.* Abingdon (1956).
A welcome attempt to find some unity in Biblical theology.
Richardson, A. *An Introduction to the Theology of the New Testament.* S. C. M. (1958).
A textbook which examines New Testament theology thematically. Not from a conservative point of view.
Taylor, V. *The Atonement on New Testament Teaching.* Epworth (1958).
An examination of the teaching from Acts to Revelation. A companion volume to *Jesus and His Sacrifice.*
Fuller, R. H. *The Foundations of New Testament Christology.* Lutterworth (1965).
A basic book for a Christology in conformity with the New Quest, but subject to the weaknesses of that quest.
Henry, C., editor. *Jesus of Nazareth, Saviour and Lord.* Eerdmans-Tyndale (1966).
A series of valuable essays from conservatives, examining the presuppositions of form criticism.
Martin, R. P. *Carmen Christi.* Cambridge U. P. (1967).
A very detailed examination of Philippians 2:5-11.
McDonald H. D. *Jesus, Human and Divine.* Zondervan (1968).
A useful brief introduction to the doctrine of the person of Christ. Conservative in approach.